Training to run the
PERFECT MARATHON

by Michael Schreiber

Illustrations by J.T. Sevier

JOHN MUIR PUBLICATIONS
SANTA FE   NEW MEXICO

Copyright © 1980 by Michael Schreiber

Library of Congress Catalogue Card No. 80-82638
ISBN 0-912528-19-2

Published by
John Muir Publications,Inc.
P.O. Box 613
Santa Fe, NM 87501

All rights reserved

First Printing September 1980

Table of Contents

Part I: Twelve Steps To The Perfect Marathon

Part II: The Race and the Rest

For Cheryl who made me do it, and tried to see that I did it right. Thanks for taking time from your own sculpting to help me sculpt this manuscript.

Thank you Ralph, Jim, Linda, Jerry and all my running friends and their families who provided companionship, friendship, moral support and lots of good times and funny stories. To Jane who encouraged me to run my first marathon and to George Kleeman, chairman of the Gulf Coast Long Distance Running Committee, who, more than anyone else, helped create the climate in which this work was spawned.

Finally, my thanks to all the people at John Muir Publications in Santa Fe: you may be slow, but you sure are good.

Michael

A Very Personal Introduction

It's a spectacle. No! It's a rite deeply rooted in our cultural past: a coming to earth of Olympian gods. Many of us had been standing enthralled for hours completely oblivious to the softly falling rain...waiting. As the heroes—men and women runners—finally flew past, great cheers went up and it was difficult to distinguish faces wet with rain from those covered with tears of joy. There appeared to be something more than human about these runners, and some of their power seemed to radiate into the crowd...we were all transformed...some for a few minutes, some for the rest of our lives.

I went home that afternoon still dazed, not quite recovered from the power that had flooded over me just a few hours before. I looked in the mirror. Still the same me—but different. My eyes seemed to have little fires in them.

I wandered around the apartment unable to focus on anything, unable to settle down. Finally I went to the closet and rummaged through some cardboard boxes stacked along the back wall. I discovered a pair of stiff old sneakers I'd been dragging around the world for years. I sat on the floor, staring at my old shoes. When I finally looked up, it was dark.

I found myself double knotting the tennis shoes. A few minutes later I was in the Ghia driving to the Rice University track.

As I stepped out onto the dark track a chill wind came up, the trees were dead still. I began to run. Faster and faster I flew around the track, the wind tearing water from my eyes and trailing it along the side of my face. A lifetime went by. Exhausted, I stopped, and stood panting in the night. Sweat poured off my body. My eyes burned from salt. I felt fantastic!

The next morning I awoke, unable to walk and hardly able to move. But I had no regrets. I knew that I was going to train and run a marathon. Look at yourself. Inside that body is a being waiting to be discovered. It takes far more than a mere human to run a 26.2 mile *Perfect Marathon* and I was to do it...so can you.

Can you really run that unimaginable distance? You bet you can! Marathons have been completed by children under ten and by men and women over seventy. They have been completed by blind people, people on artificial legs and people in wheelchairs. Marathoners have trained alone, with coaches, on teams and under the strict supervision of a doctor. But they all have one thing in common. They have all discovered a power within themselves.

The Perfect Marathon is anticipation and enjoyment that mounts slowly and steadily towards ecstacy. Training for *The Perfect Marathon* isn't always fun. You start easy, it gets harder and the deprivations can be many, but the reward is incalculable.

The power that has enabled others to run a marathon is also within you—you're about to discover it.

HOW **TO USE THIS BOOK**

Other than good science fiction, I enjoy few kinds of reading as much as a good new book on jogging and running. Such books are usually chock-full of interesting anecdotes, exciting personalities and wonderful bits of pop-psychology, and provide a delightful opportunity to miss a day of training. For that I am occasionally thankful.

As it turns out, I enjoy writing a running/jogging book as much as I do reading one.

What I hope you discover in these pages is that while running in itself really isn't all that important, life *is* important, and running can be an integral part of life.

Various sections are loaded with charts and programs, and printed charts often portray an uncompromising facade. Forget it. These programs are designed to be putty in your hands. A rock is a particularly dominating item, yet the sculptor chisels it into a form that fits. I hope you'll whack at these training schedules until they fit *your* needs.

We are all different in many important ways, but I am pretty sure that those of you who thumb through this book have at least one thing in common; either some level of interest in jogging/running or an interest in someone who jogs or runs.

If you never intend to jog a step but wish to participate as a spectator, there's a section especially for you. If you'd like to photograph a marathon, there's a section designed to help make your efforts more successful.

If you're already a marathoner of some experience and would like to improve your performance, the sections on weight training for men and women, experimentation, carbohydrate loading, nutrition, tactics and others, should be of great benefit.

If you are a person who never jogs and seldom walks, *this book is for you*! Just start at the beginning. If you are already jogging a mile or so several times a week, that's wonderful. You have already passed a major hurdle on the path to *The Perfect Marathon*. You can begin with Step One. If you are in good condition and training for a marathon, begin this program at Step Six, Seven or Eight. If you've laid off for a while, begin at a slightly earlier step.

At the ends of Steps "0" through Twelve and again at the end of "The Finish is a New Beginning," you will find charts and logs for planning your schedules and recording your progress. Please use them. Accurate record keeping is an important aspect of successful training.

During training you may encounter specifc problems: having to run in cold or rain; on sore feet; in worn-out shoes; with boredom; away from small nippy dogs. I've attempted to cover many of these contingencies, but each person has different training experiences. You will learn from your own experience and from the experiences of your running friends.

Toward the back of the book you will find the *Pace Chart*. Other books have charts using the same name, but this one works differently. There are only three columns: quarter mile; mile; 26.1875 miles.

If you are interested in finding the pace for a three hour marathon (3:00:02), find that time on the chart and move over one line to the left. A three hour marathon requires an average mile pace of six minutes and fifty-two seconds (6:52). In the first column, just left of the mile-pace, you will find that a 6:52 mile requires an average quarter-mile pace of one minute and forty-three seconds (1:43). If you plan to practice that pace on the track and want to keep yourself right-on-the-button, check your watch every loop or quarter mile.

Here is something that sounds simple but is often misunderstood. If you can run a three hour marathon you will be able to run a 1:43 quarter with ease. However, if 1:43 is your best quarter you won't have a chance in hell of running a marathon anywhere near 3:00:00. Let me go one step further. If your best mile time is 6:52 you still won't have a chance of running a 3:00:00 marathon. You'd be more likely to run it in 4:00:00. So how can you find your marathon potential? Read on.

One of the most valuable single items in this book is the Marathon Predictor. With this chart, and by controlling for certain variables, (see Tactics) you can take marathon training out of the realm of wishful thinking and make it purposeful and effective.

If your best five mile time is 35:00, that's a seven minute pace. A seven minute pace over 26.2 miles will be very close to a 3:00:00 marathon. But if you try it you probably won't even finish the race, and if you do, your time will be far below your actual potential. By using the Predictor in a creative manner, you will be able to train for and finish the marathon very close to your present potential. Even better, the Predictor will show you the pace to be run for the shorter distances in order to improve and eventually arrive at your goal.

In addition to providing training information and giving you a realistic marathon time for your state of training, the Predictor Chart also gives you a per mile pace for the target race and accumulated time for five, ten, fifteen, twenty and twenty-five miles. It takes about a year to build the *training cake*, the Predictor provides the icing.

I hope this book serves you well as a training tool. Even more, I hope you will have fun reading it and that in some way it will help further enrich your marathon experience.

Twelve Steps To The Perfect Marathon

Getting Your Feet Wet

Before beginning, take careful stock of yourself. You're probably out of condition, and many of you will be overweight.

Preparation: Getting Your Feet Wet. Welcome to the great American majority. If you have any medical problems or doubts whatsoever, check with an athletically oriented doctor. You may be asked to take a *Stress Test*, and the doctor may want to monitor your early training. Take the doctor's advice. In many parts of the country there are doctors closely associated with Cardiovascular Fitness Projects and Labs.

This book has been designed to help you avoid undue stress and lead you forward while skirting injuries. Being extremely overweight puts a great deal of strain on joints and ligaments. It's this kind of strain you want to avoid during the early months of training. If you are really overweight, try to take a little weight off at the start. You can also remain at the exercise level of Weeks One and Two for a longer period of time—until you are more comfortable with yourself.

If you are only moderately heavy, you can start right out—but only you and your doctor can really be the judge.

An easy way to lose weight early in training is to cut back on fats, eliminate foods with added sugar and eat more green salads without dressing. If you're a carnivore like me, this is a kind of good news/bad news joke. I love spareribs, so cutting out fat isn't so wonderful. But salads are my favorite, so no problem there. It evens out.

When I was in Italy a few years back making films, a diet of homepressed olive oil, marvelous pasta and wine ballooned my weight to over 200 pounds. At six feet I wasn't exactly a blimp, but I sure felt like one . . .and that was not the way I wanted to feel. Unable to sleep one night, I stumbled out of bed at 2 a.m. bloated as a milk-fed piglet. 'Enough is enough,' I thought to myself, 'things have got to change!'

Still mostly asleep, but none the less resolute in purpose, I trudged down to the nearby beach and began to run barefoot through the soft sand. As I ran, I could feel the fat melting . . .from my mind.

I have no idea how far I ran, but by the time I jogged back to the house, the first rays of sun were ginning to light the Adriatic Sea.

That morning jog marked a turning point.

By exercising instead of taking a pastry break, doing limbering-up movements before meals, eating half a head of lettuce a day with homemade yogurt, and staying away from oil and pasta, I was able to get my weight down to 185 in about a month. I wasn't to become a runner for many more years, but *something* had begun.

Once I got into marathon training, weight was no longer a problem. In fact I had to up my intake of dark beer, homemade bread and an occasional chocolate chip cookie just to keep my weight above 160 . . .Now I also get to eat a lot of ice cream . . .there are many different rewards to this marathon business.

The changes that are going to happen to you as you begin to train will be almost unbelievable. However, they take place so gradually you'll probably forget what you were actually like before you began. Have a good friend take a nude ''before'' picture of you, stick it away somewhere, and forget about it.

Remember that photo you forgot about? Good. Before you begin the program, make a note of your resting pulse rate and your morning weight on the back of that photo. You can most easily find your pulse on the inside of the wrist below the thumb, or alongside the neck just down from the ear. The pulse is taken by counting against a stopwatch. When you take your pulse at the track (which will be covered in a later section of the book), you measure only for ten seconds and then multiply by six. In the morning, take a full minute count. Why the difference? In the morning we are taking a resting rate; at the track we are measuring the rate after exercise. If we count for over ten seconds, the heart begins swiftly, begins to slow down, and we don't get an accurate measurement.

By keeping a record of the resting pulse rate, we will have a good indication of increasing fitness. My experience is pretty typical. Before I began training, my pulse was in the low 70s. After training for awhile it dropped to the low 60s and finally into the low to middle 50s. Now, when I'm working towards a marathon, my pulse goes down into the 40s. Some trained marathoners have resting pulse rates in the 30s.

Another way to measure increasing fitness is to take your pulse immediately after running, and again at five minute intervals. An increasingly fast drop in heart rate is a measure of improving condition. As time passes you should find your pulse drops from a working rate of 140 and above, to 100 beats per minute and below in an ever shorter period.

Pulse rate and recovery rate are clear-cut ways to continually gauge your progress; but to be used successfully, you must have records.

Like pulse, weight can be a ''fitness indicator.'' Lighter bodies, assuming equal training, can go further and faster on less energy than ones burdened with even a little extra fat. However, not all weight loss is good. Rapid and drastic loss, especially during the summer, may signal dehydration. By keeping weight records, you can spot a potentially dangerous case of dehydration before it gets out of hand.

For the most accurate readings, weigh yourself in the morning . . .take a trip to the bathroom, but before you have anything to eat or drink. In hot humid climes it's also a good idea to weigh yourself again after training runs to see what you are losing through perspiration. During Texas Gulf Coast summers I lose about three-quarters of a pound for every moderate mile I train. A couple of beers and a quart or two of grapefruit juice puts it right back on. If I lose much more than that, I'll cut back on training the following day and drink extra liquids.

Careful record keeping is one of the most important aspects of successful training. With properly kept charts you can plan programs, guard against over-training, spot potential injuries before they happen and, most importantly, stop training goof-offs from piling up. At the end of this step you will find a chart you can use to record daily pulse, weight, time or distance, subjective comments and weekly totals.

On the subject of totals: in our culture the mile has a great deal of symbolic meaning. *Next door, around the corner, only a few blocks, over there:* these distances sound manageable. A MILE, however, is REAL DISTANCE. For most people even the thought of running a mile is out of the question, and rightly so. Therefore your first hurdle will be to *conquer that formidable distance,* and running your first mile will remain probably one of the more significant accomplishments of your life.

Since the distance is so formidable, we will approach the mile by ignoring it altogether. We start by loosening up. You may have favorite exercises for stretching your leg and back muscles. Here are a few I use. First there's the *hamstring stretch,* better known as the toe touch. Next is the *calf stretch*—two ways to do this, both are good and both can be used in the same session. Get up on a step or a thick board and let your heels hang down. Your heels should drop low enough for you to feel a very definite stretch in your calf muscle. Don't bounce. Go up and down slowly. Stretch one calf muscle at a time or both at once. Another *calf stretch* is to do a flat-back, heels-on-the-ground pushup against a wall. This gets both calves at one time. To concentrate on a single calf, step forward with the opposite leg, keeping the working leg relatively straight and the foot and heel flat on the ground. Next we have the *Quad Stretch.* The quadriceps are those muscles on the front of your leg above the knee. Standing comfortably, grab your ankle or foot. Pull until your heel touches or gets close to your butt. Keep your back fairly straight and adjust your position so you feel the most pull in your upper leg.

Running tends to work back muscles to the detriment of stomach muscles, so we are going to have to do some work on the tummy (or gut in some cases). *Sit-ups* are great for the upper part of the stomach. When you do them be sure to have your knees bent to take undue strain off your back. To condition the lower part of your stomach, do leg raises. Keep your back flat on the ground, and don't lift your back and shoulders at the same time as you lift your legs.

To add a little variety and for people who find sit-ups uncomfortable, try knee-ups. This requires a chinning bar. (You can buy doorway models at sporting goods stores.) Hang at arms' length, and draw up your knees smoothly toward your chest. Only do a couple of these the first day, or the next morning you won't even be able to cough . . .the knee-up is a tough one that doesn't *seem* tough.

With all these exercises the important thing is to start with only a few movements and work up slowly over a period of a week or so. Avoid straining, swinging, and short choppy movements. Above all, be especially careful of anything that stresses your lower back.

Rather than having one big workout, I generally do exercises several times in the morning and evening. I do leg stretches before and after all training runs. I'll go through them in order, then keep repeating the cycle for five to ten minutes.

If you really want to get into stretching and limbering, pick up a little paperback on yoga (most book stores have a half dozen to choose from) or even join a class long enough to learn the basics. But if you just want to get on with running, the exercises I've outlined will do just fine.

Stretching, limbering and warming-up are not going to take much of your time, but they're very important. Remember, running toughens and shortens leg and back muscles. Stretching these muscles and working the stomach muscles with bent leg sit-ups, knee-ups and leg raises will go a long way toward cutting back the risk of injury . . .but we don't want the stretches themselves to cause injury.

In this game no points are given for pain and soreness, so do only about 5 minutes of easy stretches and a few sit-ups morning and evening. If you do much more at first, you may find it impossible to walk upstairs or straighten up after you tie your shoes. (For more advanced exercises, see chapter on ''Supplementary Training.'')

Our training day always starts with the stretches. *The Perfect Marathon* training week begins any day you wish to begin and continues for seven days. To keep things simple I like to work in four week segments and let the months take care of themselves. Is today the day you want to begin your first week? All right, here we go.

Week One: Step 0 Early in the morning and again in the evening (either before dinner or a couple of hours after) do 5 minutes of stretching and a few bent-leg sit-ups. Repeat this on a daily basis throughout the week.

The Perfect Marathon — Part I

Sometime during the day, possibly when the coffee and doughnut cart comes by at work, go outside and take a brisk, nonstop ten-minute walk.

On the second day pass up the doughnuts again and go out for another brisk ten-minute walk. On the third day allow yourself to quietly snicker at the people still munching those greasy rings, and go out to walk just a little longer than ten minutes.

Each day increase your time until by the seventh day you are taking a brisk fifteen minute walk.

After one week in your new lifestyle, what will you have accomplished? Seven brisk, healthy walks, fourteen stretching and exercise sessions and a full week without doughnuts. You're a triple winner!

Week Two: Step 0 This week instead of a mere 5 minutes of morning and evening stretches do 7 minutes and maybe even *a few more just before going for your brisk walk.*

Now you don't even notice the coffee sloshers and doughnut gobblers as you head out for your fast fifteen minute walk. Each day you walk a little longer and by the seventh day you're striding out for 30 minutes.

Many runners and joggers use their lunchtime for training because 30 minutes may be a bit long for a coffee break. Some companies actually give their employees an extra half-hour for lunch if they participate in the company's fitness program. If you'd like to start such a program at your company, contact the athletic director at your local ''Y,'' or write *Runner's World* and ask about the ''Corporate Cup'' program. Tell 'um Mike sent you.

Week Three: Step 0 Do you have a stopwatch or a watch with a sweep-second hand? This week you'll need it. You'll also need to take a hard look at your old tennis shoes and begin thinking about a visit to your local jogging shop to buy the real thing.

Jogging shoes are different from other sports shoes, and they're not interchangeable. In running, the foot is repeatedly slammed into the ground, and beginning runners do a lot more slamming than those with more experience. Jogging shoes have special padding to prevent you from turning your feet and joints into jelly, heel lift to protect your Achilles tendon, and heel stabilization to protect your ankles, knees and hips.

That's a lot to expect from a shoe, so a considerable amount of engineering genius must go into design. Those snazzy *looking* items on sale at discount stores for about 10 bucks may look like the real thing, but they're not. Go to a store that specializes, talk to the experts, then buy the pair that feels the best. Prices change, but expect to pay between $20 and $60.

I began with Brooks. When the manufacturer discontinued the shoe in my width I was forced to find something new. *Runner's World* rated the Tiger Pan Am number one in rear foot stability, a major factor in preventing ankle, knee and hip problems . . . I thought I'd give it a try.

Firm! Dr. John Bandy, who helped design the sole, assured me it was firmness that gave the Pan Am stability. Not convinced, I tested the Tigers in a race. Bet you're holding your breath waiting for the judgement . . . here it is. This was the first marathon I'd ever finished completely without blisters and without any apparent impact injury.

Bill Rodgers, multiple winner of the famous Boston Marathon wears Tiger and Frank Shorter also wears them to victory. Most of my friends who are long-time runners have a selection of shoes: New Balance, Nike, Adidas, Tiger, Puma, Brooks and others. The important thing is the shoe fit you and your needs.

Before you buy, try on the shoes with the same socks you plan to train in. I use tube socks and all my female friends wear low-cuts with little fuzzy balls on the back. The fuzzy balls aren't just for cuteness. They keep the socks from slipping down into the shoes.

Once you find a pair of shoes that feels right, take a jog down the center of the store, or along the front if it is in a carpeted mall. You want to make sure the shoe doesn't slip or ride up and down at the heel. If one shoe fits perfectly but the other rides a little, and you can't find a better pair, you can snug it up with several layers of Dr. Scholl's *moleskin* applied to the sides of the offending heel (inside the shoe where it grips the back sides of your foot).

I ran my first marathon in a shoe *custom-fitted* with *moleskin* and it worked fine. I still wear that same shoe for training—with the *moleskin* in it.

Are we still at Week Three? Yes, I guess we are. This week stick with 7 minutes of morning and evening exercises and stretches. Since they're so much fun, pre-walk stretches are now probably a regular part of your workout.

With tennis shoes or, better yet, jogging shoes with laces double-knotted, head out for a few minutes of brisk walking, then break into a slow, JOG for about 30 seconds to one minute, then back to a brisk walk. Don't let yourself get out of breath. I know you want to fly, but try to hold yourself back . . .you want to "train, not strain."

As soon as you feel like you're breathing normally, JOG another 30 seconds to one minute. Now for the next ten minutes alternate slow jogging and walking. A good ratio is probably 30 seconds or more of jogging to one minute of brisk walking. Whatever is comfortable for you, as long as you don't ever allow yourself to get out of breath . . .That is a central aspect of training. After you finish the 10 minutes of jog/walking, don't sit down! Continue with a brisk 10 minute walk.

The second day of this third week is a day off. No jogging or long walks. Do your regular 7 minutes of morning and evening stretching and exercising, and you can swim or go bicycling, but rest your feet. They'll thank you for it.

I know many of you feel this is too easy, and I know others skipped ahead, or maybe did a little too much, and wound up too sore to do anything. But I won't say I told you so.

The third day of this week's routine is the same as the first. From days three to seven, begin and end the jog/walking sessions with from 5 to 10 minutes of walking, and slowly increase the period of jog/walking from 10 minutes to 15.

At the end of this week you will be doing a 10 minute brisk walk to warm-up, 15 minutes of jog/walking, and 10 minutes of brisk walking to warm-down . . .Remember to take enough time for stretching.

Week Four: Step 0 This week is a repeat of last week. Too boring! OK. You asked for it. Instead of jogging a minimum of 30 seconds before walking, this week jog a full minute. Jog/walk for a total of 15 minutes, plus the warm-up and warm-down walking of 5 to 10 minutes.

Take the second day off as before. From the third day through the seventh work up from 15 minutes of jog/walking to 25 minutes. Same warm-up and warm-down. You may want to do more than a minute of jogging before you walk, which is OK, but keep your breathing normal. If you start to breathe hard it means you are jogging too fast or too far, or both. I know it's hard because you're feeling your power, but take it easy at this stage. Finish the session with at least 5 minutes of brisk walking and some leg stretches.

That's the end of the first four week period. How do the old tootsies feel? Knees and hips OK? If you have been faithful to the schedule you should be relatively pain free, full of vim and vigor, and hungry as hell from missing all those lunches and coffee breaks. Go have an ice cream or some other treat. You deserve it! From now on the training gets a little tougher, but it's also a whole lot more fun.

Week Five: Step 0 My, how time flies when you're having fun. You're already into the second four week period. You will still be doing stretching and sit-ups, morning and evening, and several minutes of leg stretches before and after your workouts. Sound familiar? Well, that's about all that stays the same.

Are you ready? Limber up. Walk briskly for a couple of minutes. Now jog slowly for 2 minutes *or longer* and walk for 30 seconds to a minute—walk only until your breathing is normal. Repeat 2 minutes or more of slow jogging followed by 30 seconds or more of walking for a total of 15 minutes. Finish with 5 minutes of brisk walking and some leg stretches. Take a day or two off and play, but save your feet.

On day three begin upping your 15 minutes of jog/walking so that by day seven you're up to 25 minutes. Always begin and end with leg stretches and several minutes of brisk walking—don't count this as part of your jog/walking time; it's extra.

By this time, you may be able to jog more than 2 minutes at a stretch without getting out of breath. If you can, by all means do so . . .and congratulations. You are beginning to be more of a runner and less of a walker. This coming week you are going to do even better.

Week Six: Step 0 OK, this week all the extra stuff is still the same, so I don't have to mention it—unless you skipped over a few pages. If you skipped, check back.

When you go out today, jog slowly for 3 minutes before you drop into a recovery walk for a minute or so . . .whatever it takes to get your breathing back to normal. The first day you're going to keep on for 25 minutes at a jog/walking cycle of 3 minute jog/1 minute or so walking . . .plus stretches, warm-up and warm-down. At the end of the seven day period you will still be doing 25 minutes—but with a difference. You take day 2 off as always, but after that you begin raising your 3 minutes of slow jogging until by the end of the week you are doing *4 minutes or more* before you walk. Remember to keep it slow and try not to get at all out of breath. Walk as long as you must but attempt to keep it below 2 minutes.

Contrary to what many of us learned at our high school coach's knee, distance training isn't improved by breathlessness. So don't eliminate the periods of walking unless you can do so comfortably and without getting your breathing and heart rate too high. Can you carry on a conversation or talk steadily to yourself while you jog? If the answer is no, either slow down or walk.

Week Seven: Step 0 This week you can begin to think of yourself as a jogger. You have passed the test of time and your jogging periods are going to be three to five times as long as your walking periods. Do all the morning and evening stuff and all the warm-up and warm-down and stretching stuff. That stays the same, except you are probably doing a lot more sit-ups or knee-ups or leg raises.

After your stretches and warm-up walk, jog slowly as long as you are able—at least 6 minutes, but no more than 10. Follow this with up to 2 minutes of walking to recover, then repeat the cycle. Alternate jogging and walking for 30 minutes. Add your warm-up and warm-down time. Take the second day off.

Beginning with day 3 increase your period of jogging, until by day 7, you are able to jog for at least 10 continuous minutes, followed by shorter periods of walking and jogging. Not all your jogs have to be 10 minutes long, but one of them should be. A typical session this week might look like this: 5 min walking warm-up / 11 min jog / 1½ min walk / 6 min jog / 2 min walk / 5 min jog / 1 min walk / 5 min jog = 31½ min / 5 min warm-down walk / stretches.

Week Eight: Step 0 By the time I had trained for eight weeks I had gone through back pains, foot pains, knee pains, sore calf muscles, sore heels and myriad blisters on every part of my feet. Of

course, I had no coach and no one to give me advice. But I'll bet that even if I had been given valuable instruction, I probably wouldn't have taken it. More likely I would have chosen to suffer and learn from experience and finally observation . . .as I did. We all have a need, at least to some extent, to learn from our own personal experience.

While I don't expect or even want you to follow these programs to the letter, I do hope you'll take the underlying philosophy to heart.

During these first few weeks, the schedules are pretty close to what most of you should be following: some of you, because of time pressures, may have to go slower, and some may go slower because of instructions from their doctors—heart patients for example. Others with more naturally robust constitutions may be able to progress faster. Some may have come to this book with recent jogging experience, and choose to skip entire weeks of preliminary training . . .whatever is best for you as an individual is what you should be doing.

This week, after your stretches and warm-up, jog at least 10 minutes and follow with a short walk. Then repeat. Continue for 30 minutes or slightly longer. You still take the second day off to play. During the week continue to lengthen the time of one of your jogs until by the end of the week it is at least *15 minutes long*.

Any given workout should have at least two jogging sessions, even if this forces you to total more than 30 minutes. For example, you might do a 16 minute jog / 2½ minute walk / 13½ minute jog = 32 minutes, plus warm-down and stretches. Remember, even on these long jogs it's important not to get out of breath.

The Perfect Marathon — Part I

It is now long past the time you should have invested in a 1st class pair of jogging shoes. If you haven't gotten them yet, why not do so as a reward for having finished your second 4 weeks on the road to *The Perfect Marathon*.

Week Nine: Step 0 This week is *exactly* like week eight, except one day you go to an outdoor track and take your stopwatch or wrist chronometer.

Stretch, warm-up, then *slowly jog* around the track 4 times without a walking break. *Note your time as you finish the 4th lap,* but don't stop. Continue to jog slowly, walking when necessary or if necessary, until 30 or 40 minutes have passed. NOW CELEBRATE. YOU HAVE DONE IT. 4 times around a standard track is ONE FULL MILE.

You have taken the first step towards *The Perfect Marathon*. Two months ago it would have been impossible, but today that mile was pretty easy. Right! Now all you will have to do is string 26.2 of them together and you'll have it licked. It really *is* as simple as that.

Step 0 Notes

- Light warm-up and stretching movements morning and evening or before and after walking/jogging sessions.

- Begin sessions with brisk ten-minute daily walk, working slowly up to a brisk thirty-minute (or longer) walk interspersed with short periods of slow jogging.

- When possible use coffee breaks and lunch hours for some of the training sessions.

- By the end of nine weeks you should be able to jog continuously for at least ten minutes.

- Purchase a pair of jogging shoes, also known as "training flats." Look for a pair with a firm heel counter, heel lift that is about twice as thick as the padding under the ball of the foot, roomy toe box and comfortable fit . . . try on the shoes while wearing the same thickness socks you plan to train in. If possible get two pair of jogging shoes and alternate . . . this will greatly extend their useful life. To avoid injury and further extend the life of your shoes, keep the heels built-up and even use weekly applications of hot-melt glue from a glue gun.

Training Log: 7-Day/9-Week Schedule

WEEK 1

	DAY 1	DAY 2	DAY 3	DAY 4	DAY 5	DAY 6	DAY 7	7 DAY TOTAL
Daily Mileage								
Comments								
Pulse	AM | PM	AM | PM	AM | PM	AM | PM	AM | PM	AM | PM	AM | PM	WEIGHT

WEEK 2

	DAY 1	DAY 2	DAY 3	DAY 4	DAY 5	DAY 6	DAY 7	7 DAY TOTAL
Daily Mileage								
Comments								
Pulse	AM | PM	AM | PM	AM | PM	AM | PM	AM | PM	AM | PM	AM | PM	WEIGHT

19

Training Log: 7-Day/9-Week Schedule

WEEK 3

	DAY 1		DAY 2		DAY 3		DAY 4		DAY 5		DAY 6		DAY 7		7 DAY TOTAL
Daily Mileage	AM	PM	AM	PM	AM	PM	AM	PM	AM	PM	AM	PM	AM	PM	
Comments															
Pulse															WEIGHT

WEEK 4

	DAY 1		DAY 2		DAY 3		DAY 4		DAY 5		DAY 6		DAY 7		7 DAY TOTAL
Daily Mileage	AM	PM	AM	PM	AM	PM	AM	PM	AM	PM	AM	PM	AM	PM	
Comments															
Pulse															WEIGHT

Training Log: 7-Day/9-Week Schedule

WEEK 5

	DAY 1		DAY 2		DAY 3		DAY 4		DAY 5		DAY 6		DAY 7		7 DAY TOTAL
Daily Mileage															
Comments															
Pulse	AM	PM	AM	PM	AM	PM	AM	PM	AM	PM	AM	PM	AM	PM	WEIGHT

WEEK 6

	DAY 1		DAY 2		DAY 3		DAY 4		DAY 5		DAY 6		DAY 7		7 DAY TOTAL
Daily Mileage															
Comments															
Pulse	AM	PM	AM	PM	AM	PM	AM	PM	AM	PM	AM	PM	AM	PM	WEIGHT

Training Log: 7-Day/9-Week Schedule

WEEK 7

	DAY 1	DAY 2	DAY 3	DAY 4	DAY 5	DAY 6	DAY 7	7 DAY TOTAL
Daily Mileage								
Comments								WEIGHT
Pulse	AM / PM	AM / PM	AM / PM	AM / PM	AM / PM	AM / PM	AM / PM	

WEEK 8

	DAY 1	DAY 2	DAY 3	DAY 4	DAY 5	DAY 6	DAY 7	7 DAY TOTAL
Daily Mileage								
Comments								WEIGHT
Pulse	AM / PM	AM / PM	AM / PM	AM / PM	AM / PM	AM / PM	AM / PM	

Training Log: 7-Day/9-Week Schedule

WEEK 9

	DAY 1		DAY 2		DAY 3		DAY 4		DAY 5		DAY 6		DAY 7		7 DAY TOTAL
Daily Mileage															
Comments															
Pulse	AM	PM	AM	PM	AM	PM	AM	PM	AM	PM	AM	PM	AM	PM	WEIGHT

We're On Our Way

By now you can actually jog an entire mile without stopping and without breathing hard. You are among the few who can jog this distance or more, so it's OK to feel a little smug. Most people can work up a sweat just shifting their car into drive or popping a doughnut.

Now that you've had your few seconds of feeling superior, it's time to remember there are people out there, much like yourself, who have to jog two or three miles before they're even warmed up. Don't be concerned. There's an old saying that no matter how fast you go, there is always someone ahead of you and someone pulling up behind.

There's another saying among marathon runners. Don't look back. If you look over your right shoulder they'll pass you on the left. If you look over your left shoulder they'll pass you on the right. If you look over both shoulders they'll climb right over your back.

Ron Tabb, a 2:11 world class marathoner, doesn't look back. Early in the Houston Marathon Ron heard someone pounding up behind him. He gazed straight ahead, and set a 4:35 mile pace.

Don't worry about the other guy or gal. Just be concernced about yourself. Being able to jog a mile or more, you have cleared the first major hurdle to running a marathon. Please believe me.

Training can sometimes be difficult, but the marathon can be easy—exciting, challenging, rewarding, but easy. That is if you prepare for it. You want to be better than you are, and this program will help you get there.

Now we begin to string those miles together. Let's do it in style.

Since you have become a serious jogger, why not dress like one: nifty shorts, socks with maybe colorful little balls on the back, 1st class jogging shoes and a T-shirt that reads *Distance Runners Last L-o-n-g-e-r* (or your favorite slogan).

All dressed up? Now's the time to get all sweated up. From now on you should do limbering and stomach exercises and stretching every morning and evening, 7 days a week—barring sickness or injury. The sessions can be anywhere from 5 minutes to 30 minutes.

Before and after each jogging workout there should be leg and back stretches lasting at least 5 minutes, plus warm-up, warm-down and cool-off. It is extremely important to develop such habits early, long before your legs have a chance to tie-up and your back rebels.

For the next 4 weeks I recommend alternating 4 and 3 day weeks of jogging. At this stage you need frequent rest . . .but it's very important there be no more than one day off between jogs (unless you are sick or injured). Four and three day weeks mean jogging every other day. *Stay active on your days off,* but rest your feet.

If you can manage it without breathing hard, jog each session nonstop, but walk when it is really necessary. 30 minute jogging sessions may be difficult, not because of the distance, but because of creeping ennui. Half an hour is a long time to be on your feet.

	Day 1	Day 2	Day 3	Day 4	Day 5	Day 6	Day 7
Week One	20 min	off	20 min	off	30 min	off	20 min
Week Two	off	20 min	off	30 min	off	20 min	off
Week Three	30 min	off	20 min	off	30 min	off	20 min
Week Four	off	30 min	off	30 min	off	20 min	off

Try running alone to enjoy the internal dialogue; then run with friends for a change in conversation. I have several groups of friends that I run with on different days. That way my jokes, lies, gossip and general nonsense have a much greater life span.

For changes in scenery you can work out several different routes along hike and bike trails, through neighborhoods, around schools and parks. When you pick your courses don't bother to measure them. At this stage you don't have to worry about distance—just worry about keeping on your feet and moving for a specific amount of time. You've started a long range savings program, not a racing program. Right now your training is designed to add to your energy store, improve the efficiency of your cardiovascular system and get your joints used to a lot of pounding.

The reason for the alternating 4 and 3 weeks of jogging is simple. This on/off approach gives the body a chance to replenish stores of muscle glycogen (the principle muscle fuel) and to recover from stress; but the layoff isn't long enough for regression to set in.

Research has shown that training effects can continue for as long as 24 hours after strenuous aerobic exercise and that regression doesn't set in until after that period.

25

The Perfect Marathon — Part I

For some time I have been nagging you to jog slowly and not to breathe hard. It's probably about time we discussed in more detail the reasons for this suggestion.

In order for exercise to have any training effect at all, it is necessary to get the pulse rate up well above the resting state. Depending on you and your condition, that resting pulse can be anywhere from the mid 30s to 80s per minute. The training effect sets in around 120-130, if that level is maintained for approximately 30 minutes or longer.

If your pulse goes too high the exercise becomes anaerobic: your body is unable to process enough oxygen to carry on the activity and you go into *oxygen debt*. This is what happens during fast, short and moderate distance races. One of the reasons you feel so rotten after an all-out mile is because of the huge oxygen debt. A distance run requires an aerobic state, a long steady conversion of energy where the body is able to process all the oxygen it needs.

Although it differs from individual to individual, the parameters for aerobic conditioning are usually set at 120-150 beats per minute. A simple rule of thumb is: if you're jogging, your pulse is high enough; if you're breathing hard, it is too high.

Later in your training there will be periods when you will briefly exceed the 150 level, but the *average* will still be within the 120-150 range and the body will have ample time during the run to recover from the small oxygen debt.

When the pulse goes much above 150 the individual is racing rather than training. Nevertheless, jogging at this rate or higher for a *small percentage* of the total week's mileage, say 5%, can be effective. It stresses different muscles, changes stride and prepares you for racing, while allowing your average pulse rate for the entire period to remain comfortably within the 120-150 range.

Although many coaches will disagree with my early de-emphasis on speed, I think Dr. Ernst van Aaken would agree—matter of fact, it was van Aaken's idea in the first place. Speed will develop as training progresses.

Except for marathoners with years of training and experience, who want to sharpen up before a competition, the ratio of slow distance to speed should remain close to 95%/5%.

Just because 95% of your jogging should be at a relatively easy pace doesn't mean you have to get into a rut. Once you can comfortably jog at 9 minutes per mile or better, for 30 minutes or so, you can begin to vary your pace between about 7:30 and 9:15 minutes per mile. This adds variety, keeps the legs from getting tight during the run, and still averages out nicely.

Always finish your training jog/run with a couple hundred yards of speed-up followed by a slow jog to warm-down and a walk to cool-off. Then stretch.

Training should be fun and varying your pace will help make it so. In fact the Swedes have a word to describe the joy to be found in our sport: *Fartlek*/Speed Play. Let's go play.

Step 1 Notes

- Every morning and evening do from 5 to 30 minutes of stretching, limbering and stomach exercises.

- Before and after every jogging session do at least 5 minutes of leg and back stretches.

- Every jogging session should include these stages: limbering; warm-up; main workout; warm-down; cool-off; stretches.

- Jog every other day. On the off days do other forms of exercise that don't pound the joints (bike riding, swimming, etc.).

- Attempt to jog the entire session but walk for brief periods if you find yourself getting out of breath . . . you should be able to carry on a conversation while jogging.

- A prime secret of long distance training is economy. Learn to jog with a gliding motion, hardly lifting your feet from the ground. Not only will this enable you to go further (enhancing cardiovascular benefit), but it will help take stress off your feet and ankles. This running style is practically silent . . . if you can hear your feet slapping the ground, you are probably running much too hard and lifting your knees too high.

Training Log: 7-Day/4-Week Schedule

WEEK 1

	DAY 1	DAY 2	DAY 3	DAY 4	DAY 5	DAY 6	DAY 7	7 DAY TOTAL
Daily Mileage								
Comments								
	AM | PM	AM | PM	AM | PM	AM | PM	AM | PM	AM | PM	AM | PM	WEIGHT
Pulse								

WEEK 2

	DAY 1	DAY 2	DAY 3	DAY 4	DAY 5	DAY 6	DAY 7	7 DAY TOTAL
Daily Mileage								
Comments								
	AM | PM	AM | PM	AM | PM	AM | PM	AM | PM	AM | PM	AM | PM	WEIGHT
Pulse								

Training Log: 7-Day/4-Week Schedule

WEEK 3

	DAY 1	DAY 2	DAY 3	DAY 4	DAY 5	DAY 6	DAY 7	7 DAY TOTAL
Daily Mileage								
Comments								
Pulse	AM / PM	AM / PM	AM / PM	AM / PM	AM / PM	AM / PM	AM / PM	WEIGHT

WEEK 4

	DAY 1	DAY 2	DAY 3	DAY 4	DAY 5	DAY 6	DAY 7	7 DAY TOTAL
Daily Mileage								
Comments								
Pulse	AM / PM	AM / PM	AM / PM	AM / PM	AM / PM	AM / PM	AM / PM	WEIGHT

No Turning Back

If it hasn't happened to you yet, it soon will. I still remember the first time. The night was dark and moonless with stars like little chips of ice in the black sky. It had been a very hot day, so I waited until one in the morning before I walked over to the Rice University track for my run. I was feeling particularly good, so my scheduled three miles went by before I even realized it.

At about three and a half miles a cold chill went through my body and I felt myself being lifted a few thousandths of an inch above the surface of the track. I was moving at an incredible speed, but without any effort on my part. Around me I sensed an otherworldly power that seemed to be hurtling me down the track.

After the five-mile point, I slowly emerged into normal reality, completed another quarter mile, and stopped. I was not at all tired. On the contrary, I was exhilarated.

This was not the only time such a thing happened, but in future encounters the amorphous force took shape. Who knows what shape it will take for you . . . a slight prickling of the skin, a chill wind . . . perhaps a voice whispering in your ear, a chorus of cherubim or even Zeus himself down from Olympus.

My good friend Dave poo-pooed jogging for quite awhile and was sometimes miffed when I turned down dinner invitations because I felt I had to run. After several months Dave decided to take up long walks and jogs. At first only his wife was in on the secret.

It wasn't long before he was jogging a mile, then two miles without stop, and by then he was only too happy to tell us about the personal records he was breaking . . .still he wasn't *really* hooked. Then one day he walked into the office, a kind of ethereal glow emanating from his person. "Now I understand," he said. *IT* had happened.

Up till now most of our training has been off the track on unmeasured courses. The purpose has been to avoid the vicious cycle of trying to go further, faster. It is this Further-Faster cycle that most quickly ends many a running career. Even so, you'll have to get on the track or on a measured course from time to time to learn a pace and do limited speed training.

You can keep your breathing normal and still jog at greatly varying speeds. While it's true we don't want to overdo things, we also must guard against laziness. I take that back. No way you can call a jogger lazy. Let's change that to: we must guard against settling back.

Several times during this month go to the track or some course you've measured yourself, and do a few miles at your regular pace. Time yourself. Chances are it will average out somewhere between 8:30 and 12 minutes per mile. If you are between 10 and 12 minutes per mile, you should probably consider doing at least two sessions a week on a measured course and attempt to cut just a few seconds per quarter mile off your time. This won't be enough to get you breathing hard, but it will begin to get you used to a slightly quicker pace. At that schedule you should be able to take a minute off your mile time over a six week period.

If your mile pace is under 10 minutes, don't worry. You will probably get to 9 minutes without even trying. If you are jogging at an 8:30 pace, slow down a bit to see what a 9 minute mile feels like. For some joggers a constant 9 minute pace is too slow and uncomfortable. If that's true for you, try a varied pace from 8:00 to 9:15.

Week One: Step Two I hope by now the twice daily stretches and stomach exercises have become a regular part of your life pattern. I also hope you're taking the time to stretch and warm-up before your jog, and plenty of time to cool-down afterwards.

This month we are going from a 4 day/3 day schedule to a continuing 4 day routine. This is going to put added stress on your body, so it will be doubly important for you to get your muscles stretched and warmed-up before you run, and completely cooled down afterwards—before you stop or sit.

The Perfect Marathon — Part I

Regardless of your pace, 8 minutes per mile to 12 minutes per mile, don't run always at the same speed. Every once in awhile pick up the pace for a city block or two, then slow back down again . . .it'll make you feel great. Once in awhile you are going to be in such a fantastic mood that nothing will hold you back. When that happens, GUN IT and really fly, but don't stop afterwards. Jog at least long enough to come back to normal.

By the end of this 4 week period you will be jogging close to three miles per day, 4 days per week. That's real training. From experience you are probably learning how to read your body. Keep a record of your thoughts and moods as well as your training hours, weight and pulse. Not only will your comments be a great aid in training, they will also be a great source of enjoyment in future years as you relive the early struggles.

This chapter is called *No Turning Back*. You have almost reached a point where running can begin to take over a major portion of your life. If you hold at this point, the chances are you will continue running for awhile before you begin to find important (?) reasons for missing training days, or cutting back. Eventually you will probably stop jogging altogether.

If you opt to continue advancing, from this point on you are risking almost certain running addiction. As training takes up more and more of your time, you may begin to choose your friends almost exclusively from the ranks of runners—for only they understand. If your spouse/lover is not among the initiated, he/she will either have to take up the sport, become an active spectator or run the risk of having you draw away into a different world. Of course, it's not the amount of time you are able to spend with a person that's important, but the quality of that time. So I guess even runners can have a "normal life." If you're still in doubt, have your friend read this book, and hook them too.

	Day 1	Day 2	Day 3	Day 4	Day 5	Day 6	Day 7	Total
Week One	30 min	off	20	off	30	off	20	1 hr: 40 min
Week Two	30 min	off	20	off	30	off	20	1:40
Week Three	30 min	off	30	off	30	off	20	1:50
Week Four	30 min	off	30	off	30	off	20	1:50

Two of my friends with non-running wives are fortunate. In both cases the women are natural nurturers. They enjoy traveling to races, oohing and ahhing over blisters, handing out Cokes and feeding picnic lunches to herds of starving near-athletes. They also tend to be the official photographers of the group . . .some of them even jog a few times a year.

(Lately, as more and more female runners enter the ranks and get into serious participation, the slightly overweight *male* comparison—complete with first aid kit, drink bottles, extra sweat clothes and camera—has become a fixture at races around the country.)

You have read the *caveat*. The choice is yours: Dare you go on? Damn betcha you dare!

Step 2 Notes

- Do stretching, limbering and stomach exercises morning and evening. More serious joggers should now begin a program of light weight-training for the entire body.

- Stretch and do a slow warm-up jog at the beginning of every running session. Finish each session with a slow warm-down jog, several minutes of walking to cool-off and at least five minutes of stretching for the back and legs.

- The previous step required jogging every other day. This step you should *switch to 4 days of running per week*.

- As distances increase it may become boring to do all your training on a track, and you may find it more enjoyable to run on the streets, trails and at the park—or if you're fortunate, at the beach. However, it is important to learn to recognize a running pace. Time yourself on a course of known distance. If you are jogging slower than 10 minutes per mile (2:30 per ¼ mile) attempt to speed up just a tiny bit; then, if absolutely necessary, walk for a brief period to get your breathing back to normal, and repeat.

- Continue to do alternate forms of non-running exercise on your off days.

Training Log: 7-Day/4-Week Schedule

WEEK 1

	DAY 1	DAY 2	DAY 3	DAY 4	DAY 5	DAY 6	DAY 7	7 DAY TOTAL
Daily Mileage								
Comments								
Pulse	AM / PM	AM / PM	AM / PM	AM / PM	AM / PM	AM / PM	AM / PM	WEIGHT

WEEK 2

	DAY 1	DAY 2	DAY 3	DAY 4	DAY 5	DAY 6	DAY 7	7 DAY TOTAL
Daily Mileage								
Comments								
Pulse	AM / PM	AM / PM	AM / PM	AM / PM	AM / PM	AM / PM	AM / PM	WEIGHT

Training Log: 7-Day/4-Week Schedule

WEEK 3

	DAY 1	DAY 2	DAY 3	DAY 4	DAY 5	DAY 6	DAY 7	7 DAY TOTAL
Daily Mileage								
Comments								
Pulse	AM | PM	AM | PM	AM | PM	AM | PM	AM | PM	AM | PM	AM | PM	WEIGHT

WEEK 4

	DAY 1	DAY 2	DAY 3	DAY 4	DAY 5	DAY 6	DAY 7	7 DAY TOTAL
Daily Mileage								
Comments								
Pulse	AM | PM	AM | PM	AM | PM	AM | PM	AM | PM	AM | PM	AM | PM	WEIGHT

Ya Can't Scare Me—I'm a Jogger

Congratulations! I knew you'd be back. Anyone who can run for a half-hour without stopping is not going to be put off by imminent divorce, desertion or general social ostracism. Would you believe that a marathon running psychologist I know claims she isn't compulsive.

We've discussed the benefits of having understanding friends and family. Even given the luck of the draw on that score, most of us still have to make some sacrifices . . .maybe give up some of the things we hold most dear. Staying in bed late, watching late night reruns on television, stuffing at the dinner table; even a few cocktail parties may have to be eliminated.

As your training sessions get longer it's going to become difficult and finally impossible to fit them into a lunch hour. At some point training will have to be switched, in part at least, to the morning, evening or both. This is not necessarily going to curtail your social life, but it sure will change it. You are going to have to get more of your kicks ''on-the-run'' so to speak.

If you are rather sloppy, as I am, in your budgeting of time, this new lifestyle is going to force you to think up a more efficient system for getting along. That's what it's done for me. I find I'm making much better use of the rest of my life. Because I know so many hours are going to be spent on the track, the road or in the gym, I must make the best use of what's left . . .or starve.

This month we are switching from a 4 day week to a 5 day week. You will notice, however, that the total time spent jogging during the first two weeks remains the same as week 4 of last month. We are attempting to get the body used to going longer distances, but without increasing weekly mileage . . .too fast.

36

	Day 1	Day 2	Day 3	Day 4	Day 5	Day 6	Day 7	Total
Week One	35 min	off	13	13	35	off	14	1 hr: 50 min
Week Two	35 min	off	13	13	35	off	14	1:50
Week Three	40 min	off	13	16	35	off	17	2:01
Week Four	40 min	off	20	16	40	off	17	2:13

How are your jogging shoes holding up? By now they should be showing some signs of wear. If you an afford it, I advise you to get a second pair. That way you can alternate shoes and give them a chance to dry out. It will make them last longer. I have another last-longer-trick. About 15 years ago, when I was into crafts and various woodworking projects, I bought a "glue-gun." I tried it out for a week and found the thing absolutely worthless . . . the plastic plugs ("hot-melt-glue") just never got really hard. Chairs with bendy joints are not that wonderful.

Fortunately, I'm a pack rat and seldom throw things away. A couple of years ago I got a flash of an idea and dug up the wonderful old "glue-gun," which has now become a Schreiber's Ace-Jogging-Shoe-Sole-Builder. What I do is wait until I can just begin to see the wear spots on the shoe—with me that's the rear outside quarter of the heel, the ball, the tip of the shoe, and slight wear just forward of the ball—and carefully fill in between the studs or patterns with the melted plastic.

This sytem has many advantages. First, it costs almost nothing. A couple of years' supply of glue sticks costs less than 6 bucks, and the life of my running shoes is extended at least 500%. More important, however, is the fact that I *never* have to run on run-over heels.

As jogging shoes wear, the hip, leg, knee, ankle and foot system is thrown progressively further and further out of line. I think it's clear that many running difficulties are caused by improper training (little warm-up and too much speed and distance too soon), and by bodily misalignment. If you take care of your shoes and do the soles before the wear is pronounced, misalignment of lower body parts will be less of a problem.

If your shoes are quite worn, you can still build them up, but be sure that you build only to

The Perfect Marathon — Part I

the level of the rest of the shoe and not beyond. Work slowly and lay the hot plastic down in small strips or swirls. As you progress come back and build up a little higher until you just reach the level you want. Don't worry if the new surface is *slightly* bumpy; it will even out during your first run.

If you have been running for awhile on worn shoes, cut back on your training for a day or so until you get used to the corrected shoes. I have been using this system for so long that I know where the soles are going to need work even before I put new shoes on. So I have gotten into the habit of filling in around the studs of brand new shoes at the projected wear points. This way the shoes wear evenly, and never have to be built up. I re-glue about every two weeks, more or less.

If you happen to kick a rock or curb, tear some stitching, or rip the fabric on your running shoes, the hot-melt-glue-gun can fix those problems as well.

Since we are on the subject of fixing problems, how are your toes? Well, I hope, and of normal color. Normal, that is, for a non-jogger.

Some of you, unfortunately, will have learned of the jogger's "trophy" called BLACK TOE. Not only does it look terrible, but it doesn't feel so hot either. The black color is blood trapped under the toenail, and is caused by continual pressure against the inside end and top of the shoe. A shoe that allows the foot to slide forward and back may also aggravate the problem.

Fortunately I've never had "black toe," but all my friends have. They suggest that there should be room between the end of the longest toe and the end of the shoe, and that toenails be kept short. Some of them also pad or tape their toes. Sounds like good advice to me, but these guys and gals still get funny looking, funny colored toes.

I have a feeling that the reason "black toe" has passed me by is because I wear shoes with a high, wide, squarish toe box.

What do you do if you get "black toe"? Wait long enough and it takes care of itself. The nail falls off. If it is caught early, a trick that some runners and podiatrists use is to burn a small hole in the nail with a red-hot wire, and let the blood ooze out. I've seen this trick performed on many occasions. I am told that it will save the nail, and after the initial shock it relieves all the pain . . .but you can't prove it by me. I pass the information on only because I've seen it done and some people swear by it (and at it). Do not consider this a personal recommendation.

If you talk to podiatrists they will tell you how this or that foot structure can lead to this or that type of malfunction. Fortunately our bodies are pretty adaptable. If your feet can take you on long pleasurable walks they will probably do the the same when you take up jogging . . .providing you wear properly maintained jogging shoes. If you have difficulties with blisters or ingrown toenails, treat them as you always have . . .after all, we aren't going to the moon, just to the track. If you have more serious problems such as pains in the feet, ankles, hips and knees that persist and won't respond to rest, stretching and exercise, head back to the podiatrist, who will probably prescribe an orthotic (custom shoe insert).

While orthotics and various types of "lifts" can compensate for many alignment and structural anomalies, they have the unfortunate characteristic of "cramming" the foot deeper into the shoe, greatly increasing the likelihood of "black toe."

Just because I've avoided "black toe," don't believe I've avoided the other ills that befall the distance runner. Far from it. I've had stress pains you wouldn't believe . . .that's why I've written the book. Maybe I'll help save you some pain.

Some of my friends feel that this book is doing a disservice. They believe that to fully understand the meaning of the marathon one must *really* suffer. My friend Jim ran his first marathon with a lifetime (not weekly, but lifetime) total of 38 miles. He *SUFFERED,* and there is no doubt that he fully understands the meaning of the marathon. Since then he has run probably dozens of 26.2 mile races, but the first few were the real tests.

Don't worry, you *will* suffer, but only in a good sense, and then only during training. The marathon, if you stick with me, should be a pleasure at the beginning and ecstasy at the end.

Step 3 Notes

- As training intensity increases, pay special attention to morning and evening stretches, limbering and stomach exercises. If you haven't yet begun a light weight-training program, now would be a good time to reconsider.

- *Switch to a 5-day per week* jogging/running program.

- Jog at a varied pace: long periods of moderate speed with short periods a little faster ... but remember to keep your breathing normal. If you're breathing hard it means you are racing rather than training. Use the "conversation test" to regulate your overall pace.

- Using a glue gun, be careful to maintain the heels of your training flats in a level condition. Run-over heels are an irresistible invitation to back, hip, knee and ankle problems.

Training Log: 7-Day/4-Week Schedule

WEEK 1

	DAY 1		DAY 2		DAY 3		DAY 4		DAY 5		DAY 6		DAY 7		7 DAY TOTAL
Daily Mileage															
Comments															
Pulse	AM	PM	AM	PM	AM	PM	AM	PM	AM	PM	AM	PM	AM	PM	WEIGHT

WEEK 2

	DAY 1		DAY 2		DAY 3		DAY 4		DAY 5		DAY 6		DAY 7		7 DAY TOTAL
Daily Mileage															
Comments															
Pulse	AM	PM	AM	PM	AM	PM	AM	PM	AM	PM	AM	PM	AM	PM	WEIGHT

Training Log: 7-Day/4-Week Schedule

WEEK 3

	DAY 1		DAY 2		DAY 3		DAY 4		DAY 5		DAY 6		DAY 7		7 DAY TOTAL
Daily Mileage															
Comments															
Pulse	AM	PM	AM	PM	AM	PM	AM	PM	AM	PM	AM	PM	AM	PM	WEIGHT

WEEK 4

	DAY 1		DAY 2		DAY 3		DAY 4		DAY 5		DAY 6		DAY 7		7 DAY TOTAL
Daily Mileage															
Comments															
Pulse	AM	PM	AM	PM	AM	PM	AM	PM	AM	PM	AM	PM	AM	PM	WEIGHT

Getting the Lead Out

When you're excited it's more fun to go fast than to go slow. There seems to be an almost universal desire to get out there on the road and haul. It's this need to *really* move that gets beginning joggers into the most trouble.

When I first started running, I'd get out on the track and run just as fast as I could. When I was completely whipped, I'd catch my breath and run as fast as I could again. I'd keep it up for miles. After a few months my body broke down.

No longer a beginning jogger, you are now a runner a good way down the path toward marathonhood. No more excuses for the dumb stuff.

Since we are training for the long run we will have to continue to pay our 95% dues . . .but that still leaves us the 5%. Last week we totaled 2 hours and thirteen minutes according to my schedule. It's possible that *you might have snuck in a few extra minutes* of training . . .I'm sure you haven't done less. Taking 5% of that total gives us very close to 7 minutes to use for speed. When we do use that time it should be on a track or on some other course that has been carefully measured.

Instead of doing the speed work on the basis of time, we will use distance: first 3/4 of a mile and then one full mile . . .Even though we call this speed work, it is still training, not racing. Run at a speed significantly faster than normal, but not all-out. When you finish you shouldn't feel like dropping down on your hands and knees and expiring. You should have enough energy left to run at least another mile at a slow jogging pace.

A speed day consists of limbering, stretching and a jog of one or more miles to fully warm-up. Then comes the speed work of from 3/4 of a mile on up to six miles, eventually followed by at least one mile of slow jogging to warm-down and a 1/4 mile walk to cool off.

	Day 1	Day 2	Day 3	Day 4	Day 5	Day 6	Day 7
Week One	30 min	20	25	(1-¾-1)	off	25	20
Week Two	30 min	20	25	(1-¾-1)	off	30	20
Week Three	30 min	20	30	(1-1-1)	off	30	20
Week Four	30 min	25	30	(1-1-1)	off	30	20

Figuring 9 minutes each for the two slow miles and 8 minutes for the fast mile, the total time for week four is: 2:46. At an estimated average pace of 9 minutes per mile, that comes out to just under 18½ miles for this week. Very Good!

For a while now, at least as far as my arbitrary schedule is concerned, the fourth day of each week will be speed day, and the fifth will be a day off. The first day will be the longest run. If this schedule doesn't work for you, feel free to advance it or pull it back, but try to keep the relationships of the days the same. For example: always have the medium runs before and after the long run and a day off after the speed run. There should also be at least a couple of days between the long run and the speed run.

Running fast is far less efficient than slow running, and *at speed* glycogen is burned up at a fantastic rate. Perhaps this isn't so very important now, when your speed day has only a single fast mile, but as your fast miles begin to pile up, glycogen depletion will become a factor. Taking a day off after the fast run gives the body a chance to make up that lost muscle fuel and recover from unusual stresses. Much later in the book we will discuss "carbohydrate loading," which is a method for packing a tremendous amount of glycogen into the muscles for a short period in preparation for the marathon.

By now you can be very proud of your achievements. You have made a number of PRs (Personal Records) and are probably more fit than 94½% of the general population of the United States. Wow! You have run your first mile without stopping. You have run 2 miles without stopping. Some of you have run 3 miles and more without stopping, and some have run a nonstop 30 minutes. GAD ZOOKS!

Do you realize that you no longer have to string 26.2 runs together. Now all you have to do is string 8.7333 runs end-on-end and you've got it. A piece of cake, right!

Given the amount of time you're spending in sweat socks, it's obvious that jogging is becoming an important part of your life. And maybe, just maybe, affecting your human contacts in some negative manner. If so, consider taking advantage of some of the social opportunities available as a part of the running scene.

Most towns have running clubs and their most popular events are usually *Fun Runs*. Fun Runs are usually held on weekday evenings or on weekend mornings or afternoons, depending on the weather. They are very informal events and generally cover all the distances from the dashes up to 3, 5, or even 6 miles.

The Perfect Marathon — Part I

Participation is usually open and kids from 7 years to 60 or 70 years take part. It's not unusual to see entire families entering as teams, or mothers/sons and fathers/daughters entering.

It really makes little difference how slow or fast you are; no one cares and in most cases everyone gets a certificate.

Fun Runs really round out a training schedule, make the time go faster, spark you up when you're down, and take the place of speed runs. Best of all, you get to meet many fantastic people with interests like your own. To find Fun Runs in your area call the local AAU, the ''Y,'' or a good sporting goods store (listed in the phone book) and ask for information on local running clubs.

Step 4 Notes

- Continue morning and evening stomach exercises and limbering program.

- Put greater emphasis on your full-body weight training program.

- Pay attention to diet and sleep patterns. Heavier exercise and increased activity put unusual demands on the body. Many joggers and runners find that they will need more sleep as they increase their training load.

- Switch to a 6-day jogging/running week (one complete day off).

- One day a week should include an extended speed run, beginning with ¾ of a mile and working up to overtime. Each training week will also include one day in which the mileage is significantly longer than the other days . . . as much as double or longer.

- Increased intensity and duration of these workouts makes your pre-run routine and post-run cool-off and stretching even more important than before.

Training Log: 7-Day/4-Week Schedule

WEEK 1

	DAY 1	DAY 2	DAY 3	DAY 4	DAY 5	DAY 6	DAY 7	7 DAY TOTAL
Daily Mileage								
Comments								
Pulse	AM | PM	AM | PM	AM | PM	AM | PM	AM | PM	AM | PM	AM | PM	WEIGHT

WEEK 2

	DAY 1	DAY 2	DAY 3	DAY 4	DAY 5	DAY 6	DAY 7	7 DAY TOTAL
Daily Mileage								
Comments								
Pulse	AM | PM	AM | PM	AM | PM	AM | PM	AM | PM	AM | PM	AM | PM	WEIGHT

Training Log: 7-Day/4-Week Schedule

WEEK 3

	DAY 1		DAY 2		DAY 3		DAY 4		DAY 5		DAY 6		DAY 7		7 DAY TOTAL
Daily Mileage															
Comments															
	AM	PM	AM	PM	AM	PM	AM	PM	AM	PM	AM	PM	AM	PM	WEIGHT
Pulse															

WEEK 4

	DAY 1		DAY 2		DAY 3		DAY 4		DAY 5		DAY 6		DAY 7		7 DAY TOTAL
Daily Mileage															
Comments															
	AM	PM	AM	PM	AM	PM	AM	PM	AM	PM	AM	PM	AM	PM	WEIGHT
Pulse															

STEP

Entering the Big Time

Boy, that was a good month! Weekly times and mileage are going up, we're doing a little speed work and it looks suspiciously as if at least one of our days is going to be l-o-n-g. We are definitely getting into the *for-real training stage*.

The brass bands are all booked up, so this month we will slip past the 20 mile per week barrier rather quietly and begin our approach to the 30 mile per week plateau.

If you have been able to follow the schedule fairly closely, I suspect your progress has probably been steady and relatively trauma-free. There are events, however, over which we have little control: family, social, business difficulties and pressures—colds, flu, rotten weather—all of which can interrupt the smooth steady march of progress.

The doctor did an examination, took some x-rays and told Jim he would probably never be able to run again. He did, however, give the downed athletic some exercises and stretches to relieve some of the discomfort.

Jim did the exercises and the stretches and continued to run despite the pain. He was in constant agony, but, except for a day off now and again, he wouldn't quit . . .What A Man.

Fortunately this suffering soul came down with one hell of a case of flu. When he recovered almost two weeks later, the back pains were gone, and he's now running from six to nine miles a day, and upping his mileage weekly. He's also playing tennis, baseball, and lifting weights.

The doctor heard about Jim's recovery and is reported to have said that the next time a fanatical runner comes into his office with a wiped-out back or other stress injury, he's going to seriously consider injecting the masochist with a load of virus . . . "That's the only way to get them off their feet!"

If outside forces have interrupted your training from time to time, but you have managed to stay on schedule by skipping steps or accelerating through them, you may be feeling some unpleasant twinges.

Normally, twinges from over-training occur in the Achilles tendon (that stringy thing that attaches your calf muscle to your heel) and various parts of your foot and ankle. Hips, back and knees are also highly susceptible.

If you have been doing most of your training on the track, one side of your body is giving you more trouble than the other, because you've been running gerbil-like in a continuous counterclockwise circle.

A beginning runner I know developed a nagging pain in one of her knees from running exclusively on the track. Her doctor suggested that she run in the opposite direction for a while. Two weeks later she had pains in both knees.

Some runners and coaches suggest running-through-pain. In most cases I think that's a "crock." If you are experiencing some slight stress pain (not discomfort, but pain), I suggest that you *immediately stop all running* for *at least a week* and switch to some *alternative exercises*. Alternative exercises are anything that will get you off your feet but will still allow you to get your heart rate well above the resting state and keep it there for a minimum of 30 minutes. Some "alternative" exercises are the half squat (partial deep knee bend—with or without weights), bicycling (stationary or road), swimming (alternating sidestroke or freestyle), and clean and press (from the floor with a light barbell). Depending on the location of your injury, you could do one or all of the above. Alternative exercises should be done 4 to 7 days a week . . .twice a day if you wish, for 30 minutes each session.

If your pain is more than slight, you should *stop running* for at *least two weeks* and go on a program of *alternate exercises*. For any serious injury, see your doctor.

Jim (whose name appears frequently in these pages) came down with a back pain you wouldn't believe. As soon as he had run only a quarter mile the back would start hurting him. Finally he went to the doctor, who told him to cut way back.

Jim laid off for a day or so, but being a superman he went right back to running and the horrible pain. Finally it got so bad he could hardly move. It was agony to sit down, agony to stand up, and real 1st class agony to walk. Jim went back to the doctor.

Have I made my point? If it hurts, get off it for a week or two and do something else.

The Perfect Marathon — Part I

When you return pain free after a week's lay off, step back at least one week in the training schedule. If you return pain free from a two week lay off, step back two or three weeks in the schedule.

This graduated program is designed in part to prevent loss of your training time due to pain and injury. Although the training pace may seem slow, it is actually much faster than a more concentrated, forced schedule that doesn't allow for delays due to loss of interest from too much pressure, exhaustion, stress pain and actual physical breakdown.

We want to prevent physical pain if at all possible. If it does occur we want to zap it before it grows and begins to screw up other body parts.

Don't just lay off for a day or so—a typical mistake that merely prolongs the agony. *Get off your feet right away* and stay off long enough to be sure the pain is really gone, then stay off a little longer.

The *alternative exercises* will help delay the regression of your fitness, but more importantly, they'll burn up some energy and keep you from climbing the walls.

Enough pain and injury, it's time for this month's work. Morning and evening stretches, limbering and sit-ups should still be an important part of your training day; and stretching, warm-up, warm-down and cool-off are still essential parts of your run.

Using the same estimate as last month, slow miles 9 minutes, fast miles 8 minutes, the schedule shows a total of three hours and thirty-nine minutes (3:39) for the fourth week. If you are holding an *average* overall pace of 9 minutes per mile, this week we have covered over 24½ miles. That's a lot. Even more fantastic is your long run of 45 minutes. That's 5 miles nonstop—great work. I bet you just can't wait for the new heights you're going to reach next month.

This coming month not only will we crash through new barriers and establish fantastic new PRs (Personal Records), but we're going to drastically change the training routine. Can you believe that some of our runs will actually be shorter than they are now? Well, it's true. Just wait and see.

	Day 1	Day 2	Day 3	Day 4	Day 5	Day 6	Day 7
Week One	35 min	25	35	(1-1¼-1)	off	35	20
Week Two	40 min	25	35	(1-1¼-1)	off	35	25
Week Three	45 min	30	35	(1-2-1)	off	35	30
Week Four	45 min	35	35	(1-2-1)	off	35	30

Step 5 Notes

- 10 to 30 minutes of exercising and stretching morning and evening. Some runners get together a couple of times a week and make this a social event.

- At each step training involves either greater time or greater intensity. This challenges your body in new ways, making it increasingly necessary to learn to "read your body" to become aware of the subtle difference between discomfort and pain.

- In general, if discomfort remains at a low level or decreases during training, continue. If discomfort increases during a run, it's a signal to slow down or stop for a short while and try again. While you may attempt to run through discomfort, *don't attempt to run through pain*.

- At this stage, what causes discomfort or pain? Increasing mileage too fast; increasing mileage and speed at the same time; running too hard—pounding with the feet; doing most of your longer mileage around a track—the curves'll get you; running long or fast mileage on run-over heels; switching from a soft running surface to a hard one, and surprisingly, switching from a hard to a soft surface . . . CHANGE IS WHAT GETS YOU!

- If you're feeling discomfort that is more than casual, analyze the above; pay special attention to post-run cool-off and stretches; and make sure your running shoes haven't worn over.

- If you're feeling pain that gets worse while you train, STOP running and *do some other form of exercise* that doesn't affect the painful area. If a week or two of rest (continue your stretches and stomach exercises if possible) doesn't affect a cure, see your DCM, DPM or MD. Most problems cure themselves with just a little rest, exercise and some slight modifications in training. Some don't cure themselves and require adjustments such as heel lifts, orthotics, dietary changes, and/or medical intervention. For more detailed discussion, see "Cures For Common Running Injuries" by Steven I. Subotnick, DPM.

Training Log: 7-Day/4-Week Schedule

WEEK 1

	DAY 1	DAY 2	DAY 3	DAY 4	DAY 5	DAY 6	DAY 7	7 DAY TOTAL
Daily Mileage								
Comments								
	AM | PM	AM | PM	AM | PM	AM | PM	AM | PM	AM | PM	AM | PM	WEIGHT
Pulse								

WEEK 2

	DAY 1	DAY 2	DAY 3	DAY 4	DAY 5	DAY 6	DAY 7	7 DAY TOTAL
Daily Mileage								
Comments								
	AM | PM	AM | PM	AM | PM	AM | PM	AM | PM	AM | PM	AM | PM	WEIGHT
Pulse								

Training Log: 7-Day/4-Week Schedule

WEEK 3

	DAY 1	DAY 2	DAY 3	DAY 4	DAY 5	DAY 6	DAY 7	7 DAY TOTAL
Daily Mileage								
Comments								
	AM | PM	AM | PM	AM | PM	AM | PM	AM | PM	AM | PM	AM | PM	WEIGHT
Pulse								

WEEK 4

	DAY 1	DAY 2	DAY 3	DAY 4	DAY 5	DAY 6	DAY 7	7 DAY TOTAL
Daily Mileage								
Comments								
	AM | PM	AM | PM	AM | PM	AM | PM	AM | PM	AM | PM	AM | PM	WEIGHT
Pulse								

Time to Split

In marathon training certain things are sacred: the long (l-o-n-g) run, the speedy day and the day off.

Moderate length, daily runs will get you into superb condition, but only periodic runs of exceptional length will adequately prepare you for the *Marathon Distance*.

A couple of years ago when we were training for the Dallas White Rock Marathon, the *King Kongs* would meet every Sunday morning for a weekly 20 miler. At least three people took part in every run, and someone would always try to talk us out of going the entire 20 miles. "What's so magic about 20 miles?" was a familiar moan. "So we go 15 miles, that's a great run...it won't make any difference if we miss just one twenty!" The answer, of course, is, if you miss one 20 you miss two, then three and finally you don't do any at all. Fortunately the positive (compulsive) types always outnumbered the others, so we got our miles in. It's interesting that often the previous week's would-be malingerer would be the next week's *true believer*.

During that period members of the team were averaging between 45 and 80 miles per week. As you can see we were at various individual stages of development, but we all had the 20 milers in common.

54

During the weekend runs we came in contact with other marathoners who were racking up high weekly totals but were limiting their long runs to 12 or 15 miles, with maybe an 18 miler thrown in for good luck.

On marathon day, many of the high-weekly-mileage/no-long-run people failed to finish and others finished in great discomfort. The ones that did finish tended to be those that had done at least one 18. What about the *King Kongs*?

We may not be great runners (for sure we're not), but we all put in at least three 20 milers before the marathon. We all established new Personal Records during the event, and we were all able to return to a high level of training two days later. In my case, after running the marathon on Saturday I took Sunday off and ran a slow, easy 15 miles on Monday. This would not have been possible without the weekly l-o-n-g ones.

Besides the long-run day, the other two inviolate days are the speedy day and the day off.

A few faster than normal runs over medium distances will teach you to recognize a marathon pace and accustom your body to the slightly longer stride and somewhat different stresses encountered in the racing situation. For example, after a fast run you may notice a tight or congested feeling high in the back muscles of your upper legs and in the muscles of your butt. This is caused by a change in stride and body position during speed.

Because of the tightening effect of speed work, pre-warm-up and post-warm-down stretching become even more important than before. At this stage if you forget and cut back on the limbering, you will be asking for real trouble…pulled muscles you *will* get.

The day off following the fast day is essential to prevent creeping exhaustion and staleness. I sometimes take *two* day's rest during a week, but this necessitates much longer distances on the remaining days in order to keep my total mileage up.

Not everyone agrees about rest days. One acquaintance runs as many as 150 miles per week. When he's feeling poorly from a cold or injury, his idea of cutting back is 120 miles per week! Not too long ago a combination of factors caused him to miss training (something that almost never happens). Right afterward he entered a race.

"I felt at least 10, no, 20 years younger," he told me. "It was the first time I had ever entered a competition rested." A week or so later he was back up to 120 miles per week.

He's 50 years old. "I know I'm training too much," he confesses, "but I can't help it. I have to run! I'm going to stop running the marathon, though. I guess it just isn't my event. From now on I'll

concentrate on the ultras: 50 and 62½ mile events probably suit my personality better.'' He now runs the ultra-marathon and is doing even better than he did at the mere 26.2 mile distance.

Now that we've gotten past the sacred days, the remaining days of the week are yours to play with, with two provisos. First, no single run should be less than 2 miles or 18 minutes, plus the few minutes of warm-up and warm-down. Second, your weekly total mileage or time should be consistent with that suggested in the schedule.

This month our chart will look slightly different. In addition to the daily times/mileage there will be other times. These are to provide for *split-days*. Don't confuse *split-days* and *split-routines* with ''splits.'' ''Splits'' are cumulative times given at various points in a race. In a marathon you may, for example, get ''splits'' at 1 mile, 5 miles, 10, 15, 20 and 25 miles.

Sometimes your schedule will call for, or you may feel you need for, a given mileage for a day, but you just can't spare the time in one lump. Or perhaps it's very hot and muggy and you don't feel like slogging. In such cases you may opt for 2 miles before breakfast and 4 miles instead of lunch, or 3 miles in the morning or noon and 3 miles in the evening. Again I must emphasize that split-training should be used only for ordinary days. The long run and the speed run should never be split!

There's no requirement to use the added time (indicated in parenthesis with a + sign at the end of each week) in the form of a split-day. You can add the time directly to a training run. The decision is yours. Whatever your decision, avoid making consecutive training days the same length. Varied days seem to be easier on both mind and body.

Use bracketed [+ time] as you like, when you like.

	Day 1	Day 2	Day 3	Day 4	Day 5	Day 6	Day 7	
Week One	50	35	35	(1-1½-1½)	off	35	30	[+18 min]
Week Two	50	33	33	(1-1½-1½)	off	35	30	[+20, +20]
Week Three	50	31	35	(1-1¾-1½)	off	38	30	[+18, +20]
Week Four	55	35	35	(1-2-1)	off	40	30	[+20, +20]

Our time for the final week of this chart is 4:29. Converted to miles it is 30 Big Ones…that is if you have been averaging 9 minutes per mile or a little better.

A further note on the added split-day times. If you choose not to use some of them as split-days, but wish to add them to a regular run, it's not necessary to add the entire lump to a single run. You can spread the time around.

If you choose to go the split-workout route, either use one of the listed times as is or add it to a day's run, then split the run any way you wish (as long as all single runs are 18 minutes or longer.) An example: on week one, day six, you might run 18 minutes in the morning and 35 in the afternoon. Or you might add the two together for 53 minutes which you could divide into a 25-minute morning run and a 28-minute evening run. Lots of possibilities.

As you become more experienced at running, the opportunities for creative training expand delightfully.

I know many couples where one runner is much further along in training than the other, and is able to run at a faster pace without exceeding a target pulse rate. Because they enjoy each other's company they jog together for several miles, and then continue their training either alone or with friends of similar ability.

Jogging has become so much of a family affair that it is no longer unusual to see three generations hitting the trail together. These family runs of grandparents, parents and grandchildren often culminate in picnics, cookouts and greater understanding between the generations.

Fun Runs, especially if held in a public park, almost always turn into a gigantic party of some sort.

A friend and I are looking for a nice stretch of country road, at least partially wooded, so we can take an all-day 30 mile jog. Family and other interested parties will follow in a couple of campers providing us with stuff to drink. Those that feel like it can jump down and jog for as long as they want, then get back in the bus to laze around. Some may bring bicycles. At the end of the day we'll have a campfire cookout and a keg of beer…now that's what I call creative training.

Step 6 Notes

- Long-term jogging tends to shorten leg muscles and, if the stomach isn't in shape, puts some extra strain on the back. So . . . at this level of training, morning and evening limbering movements to keep the body supple, and stomach exercises to take stress off the lower back are especially important. Try to devote a minimum of 15 minutes per session.

- Step 6 requires a six-day training week with one full day off. The training will be designed along a double hard/easy system. On one level this will consist of a long slow run, a short swift run, moderate runs, and a full day off.

- Within the context of the moderate distance runs you should also use the hard/easy or short/long system. For example, instead of running two consecutive 5-mile days, run a 6-miler and a 4-miler. Even though the total mileage is identical, the training effect will be greater and the negative stress much lower. Six miles causes the body to adapt to a higher level of stress and the 4-miler allows the body to recover.

- Split days are another way to add mileage while providing recovery periods. In this step's training chart, time (in brackets) is to be added to daily mileage as you see fit. It may be used to extend a single daily run or to create additional daily training sessions—split training days. On split days, one of the runs should be long and the other short enough to allow for recovery—but no shorter than 3 miles or 30 minutes.

Training Log: 7-Day/4-Week Schedule

WEEK 1

	DAY 1		DAY 2		DAY 3		DAY 4		DAY 5		DAY 6		DAY 7		7 DAY TOTAL
Daily Mileage															
Comments															
Pulse	AM	PM	AM	PM	AM	PM	AM	PM	AM	PM	AM	PM	AM	PM	WEIGHT

WEEK 2

	DAY 1		DAY 2		DAY 3		DAY 4		DAY 5		DAY 6		DAY 7		7 DAY TOTAL
Daily Mileage															
Comments															
Pulse	AM	PM	AM	PM	AM	PM	AM	PM	AM	PM	AM	PM	AM	PM	WEIGHT

Training Log: 7-Day/4-Week Schedule

WEEK 3

	DAY 1	DAY 2	DAY 3	DAY 4	DAY 5	DAY 6	DAY 7	7 DAY TOTAL
Daily Mileage								
Comments								
Pulse	AM | PM	AM | PM	AM | PM	AM | PM	AM | PM	AM | PM	AM | PM	WEIGHT

WEEK 4

	DAY 1	DAY 2	DAY 3	DAY 4	DAY 5	DAY 6	DAY 7	7 DAY TOTAL
Daily Mileage								
Comments								
Pulse	AM | PM	AM | PM	AM | PM	AM | PM	AM | PM	AM | PM	AM | PM	WEIGHT

The Great Plateau

When I was struggling toward my first marathon, a guy designed a program for me that he guaranteed would get me through the 26.2 miles in good shape and within a specified time. Of course that time was arbitrary, and much later I found out that the guy wasn't *really* a marathoner.

In any case, the schedule he burdened me with was *graven in stone*. Each week the total mileage went up at an exact rate, the long run went up at an exact rate, and although the fast run stayed the same length from week to week, it got faster and faster at a predetermined rate…there was absolutely no relief from the pressure.

At first the schedule was a challenge, and I smugly stayed just ahead of the miserable distances and times. No trouble during the first weeks. I was feeling invincible. Then one late afternoon, as I was finishing my six miles in record time, I realized that no matter how well I did, the damn schedule would require me to do even more the following week…*Pause for thought*…'That coming weekend I'd do my long run knowing that the next one would have to be both longer and faster, and following that there would be another weekend run yet faster and longer'…my spirit was going.

It was a Sunday morning less than two months from the target marathon when I stopped in the middle of my run and said, ''The Hell With It! Who *needs* to run a marathon! The training is a bore! The race itself will be hellish.'' I decided never to run again and, true to my word, three weeks later I still hadn't run a step. Than an anonymous postcard arrived reading *To Be Or Not To Be A Marathoner.* The next day another card arrived *Now Or Never,* and the next day still another *You Can Do It.* Then there was a message on my answering service to call a certain number that I didn't recognize. I called back. It was Ralph Nolte, a marathoner of many years' experience who I had met at the track.

Ralph, a soft spoken, normally even-tempered guy, really tore into me. I almost didn't recognize him. He called me every kind of a bum you can imagine and didn't let up even then. Ralph doesn't use four-letter words, so you can see the fantastic level of his vocabulary when you realize that 10 minutes later he was still dumping a load on me and hadn't been forced to dip into the Anglo-Saxon…''and you'll be at the track this evening to train,'' he finished. ''I'll start back in the morning,'' was my feeble reply. ''Too late,'' bellowed Ralph, and Ralph isn't one to bellow casually. ''Be there this evening!''

The Perfect Marathon — Part I

Not only was I on the track that evening, but I was back training again the next morning as well. I knew there wasn't enough time left to train properly, but I decided to do my best. And I did. Over a three-week period I took 40 training runs, doing split days almost every day, and three runs on occasion. But even this wasn't to be enough.

My longest week before the race was not very long, and I hadn't run a twenty miler in months.

I had no real idea of what finish time to shoot for, and although I had heard about pacing, I was without experience and no one I knew stressed its importance.

The day before the race, my engine blew up and I had to be towed with a nylon rope for almost 30 miles to the town where the marathon started. Needless to say, I was less than calm and had trouble sleeping that night. The mishap didn't do Ralph much good, either. He was the one who had towed me for two and a half hours.

Hard to believe, but I felt wonderful at the start of the race and naturally started much too fast. By the first mile I was well ahead of schedule (a bad sign), and by mile five I was even further ahead (a worse sign). At mile six I was hit by a stabbing pain in my gut that doubled me right over. *Now* I know this was a direct result of blasting out too fast too soon.

The pain forced me to walk, clutching my stomach. Hundreds of people passed me by. I thought I'd have to drop out, but by rubbing, and breathing slowly, the pain went away and I was running again…fast. I passed most of the people who had passed me, and I was feeling wonderful…laughing and joking. I hadn't learned my lesson at all.

The pain hit again around the eleven or twelve mile mark. I was bent over again, but I didn't stop. With one hand I massaged my stomach and with the other I pinched my upper lip. This acupressure trick took the pain away and I was off at full speed again.

My early pace, short training weeks, and training without long runs, finally took their toll. I had really trained for only a 15 mile race. As the twenty-two mile mark approached I was so tired I was whimpering and swore marathons were an abomination. I'd never run one again! Boy was I dragging.

Less than a half mile from the finish line I heard someone call my name and the world changed for me. I was no longer tired. I stood up straighter and began to pick up speed. Ralph's daughter came out on the course to run with me. I was going faster. During the last two hundred and fifty yards I whipped past other runners; so fast it seemed as if they were going backward, and during the last hundred yards I was planning my training for the next marathon, a scant four weeks later. In my mind, this was a perfect finish, and the next race was to be a *Perfect Marathon*. I was hooked…a full blown addiction according to Glasser.

As part of my addiction, especially since entering marathons, I've read many of the popular books and studies on our sport. Most have been interesting, and the anecdotes are often delightful. If you love the sport you'll love the books too, and they are great for whiling away time when it's too stormy to run. Unfortunately, because of content or organization problems, most are not very practical training tools. There are several notable exceptions, and two that have been most valuable to me.

Cooper's *Aerobics* books started the whole movement, and they are a delight to use, especially for the beginning jogger. I do take exception to an apparent emphasis on gaining points through speed rather than extended distances, but this probably results from Cooper's realistic appraisal of how much time most people actually have available for training purposes. As you know by now, my feeling is that the quickest path to pain is speed. I own all of Cooper's books, but if I were to choose the most valuable one for beginning male and female joggers, it would be *Aerobics For Women*. I love the chart for converting pie to aerobic points!

The book that has most affected my philosophy of training is *The van Aaken Method* by Ernst van Aaken, M.D.

The Perfect Marathon — Part I

Dr. van Aaken believes in running easy and far, at a speed and in a manner that makes the activity joyful. Run in the woods and in the park. Run slow and enjoy nature. Stop and have a drink of water. Stretch a little and run some more. "Run like a child runs." Cover 20 miles, but take half a day if necessary to do it. I like his style! Let's use it in our push from 30 to 40 miles per week.

This is Step Seven, and we are beginning this step having trained nearly 30 miles per week on two consecutive weeks. By the end of this step we will be at the 40 mile per week level. 35 to 40 miles is *The Great Plateau*. I see no reason for exceeding that mileage unless you are making a final surge toward the marathon.

40 miles is a lot of miles, and the longer you remain within the 35-40 range (with occasional dips to 30 or even a bit lower) the better you'll be able to withstand the rigors of final marathon preparation.

During these coming weeks, it's really your decision how you finally arrive at 40 miles.

It is extremely important to have a long day of up to 7 miles and another day when you do a few miles faster than normal. It is also important to take at least one day off, two days if you are getting over-tired. It is important to *learn to read your body*.

If you're feeling hung over from training or remain heavy-legged the day after a run, it's a sure sign to cut back, change your schedule, look at your diet and sleep patterns, and maybe get in a whirlpool with a cold glass of mineral water. Don't let the negatives build up on you. Make changes or seek remedies and and see them through.

I am again including a schedule with this step. It will provide you with a framework to amend or flesh out as you will.

It is possible, even likely, that many of you have been held back or forced to retrench because of outside pressures and/or second thoughts. Some of you may not yet be at the 30 mile level. That's fine. The program is flexible enough to take all these factors into consideration. Proceed at your own speed, but avoid disappointment by training no less than three times per week for at least 30 minutes per session. Remember, this is a bare minimum. When you reach 30 miles per week hold it for a couple of weeks or until you feel you're ready, then venture forth on Step Seven.

If you are at 30 but find going to 40 in 4 weeks is too fast, take a couple of extra weeks to do it.

As before, the times in brackets on the charts are to be used as split-days (two or more runs per day), or added to the regular training days as you wish.

The times in brackets can be used as extra runs, can be added to one or more existing runs, or added to one or more runs and divided as wished.

	Day 1	Day 2	Day 3	Day 4	Day 5	Day 6	Day 7	
Week One	55	32	33	(1-2-1)	off	40	30	[+25, +25]
Week Two	60	36	36	(1-2-1½)	off	40	30	[+42, +30]
Week Three	65	36	36	(1½-2½-1½)	off	40	32	[+45, +35]
Week Four	70	40	35	(1½-2-2)	off	45	33	[+45, +45]

This step finishes with a week's total of approximately 40 miles, and an average of 9 minutes per mile; our weekly long runs look (rounded off) like this: Week One 6 miles, Week Two 6½ miles, Week Three 7¼ miles, Week Four 7¾ + miles. This is a fairly gradual increase that should cause no difficulties, especially if you are conscientious about taking the off day at least once a week. If you are training in hot weather, stop halfway through the long run for a drink of water and stretch. As the long runs get longer you may be stopping for water three or four times. Remember this is training and not racing, and stops for water and stretches actually improve the training effect.

The lengths of the long runs may be going up too fast for some. In that case, spread the increases out over a few more weeks. If the increases seem too slow for you, don't fool yourself…after this point they really start building up fast, so try to rein in your enthusiasm.

I suspect the most difficult part of this month's program is finding the time to run, and the mental strain of spending so many *hours* jogging.

By now you realize the importance of putting variety into your training. If you've been jogging in well-frequented areas, no doubt you've met many pavement and track-pounders like yourself. Take full advantage of those acquaintances and make new friends to run with.

If you plan to take a trip, nothing's to stop you from parking your car in some new area and going on an exploratory jog. If you want to do a superficial freshen-up after such an outing, pre-moistened towelettes are very refreshing. For a more thorough washing you can use public facilities or the restroom in some restaurant or gas station. A few patrons may be put off, but what the heck.

Another approach to variety that can be a lot of fun is jog/biking. It takes two people and one bike. Both start at the same time, one on foot and the other on a 10-speed (with plenty of water on the rack).

The Perfect Marathon — Part I

After some predetermined distance, the biker stops, takes a drink, locks the bike and begins to jog. When the person who started out jogging reaches the bike, he or she takes a drink, does some stretches and does the next leg on wheels…you meet your friend in passing. This goes on as long as you wish, but be sure that you have two keys to the bike lock (or combination) and that you turn around at some time so you can get back to your car before you hit an ocean or an international border. A slight variation on this is for the bike rider to leave 10 or 15 minutes after the jogger has started. Of course, two people can jog and bike side-by-side.

Now that we've been able to figure ways of getting in the miles without losing our minds or families, you will be delighted to hear that for the time being at least, our *weekly mileage* will no longer be going up and some *daily mileage* will be going down. Before you breathe a sigh of relief, be forewarned that the mileage missing from some daily runs will be added to the l-o-n-g run. For some this new plan will be much easier to cope with. Do a bunch on one day, and you can look forward to some lighter days the rest of the week…slim consolation, huh!

Step 7 Notes

- Consistency is one of the most important ingredients in successful training. No matter if you exercise 5 to 10 minutes or 30 to 40 minutes per day; no matter if you are jogging 2 to 4 miles a day or running 10 to 12 miles a day; you will achieve the greatest results and the fewest injuries if you are consistent—NO EXTENDED LAYOFFS. This does not apply to pain or injury-related layoffs.

- Consistency also requires the avoidance of abrupt changes and compulsive pressure to increase training volume and intensity: Do not increase mileage or speed at a steady unrelenting rate. Set reasonable goals but give yourself a chance to retrench. Push forward, of course, but also take a breather from time to time. Jogging, running and racing should be a challenge . . . and fun.

- This step has brought us to the 40 mile per week level, and during the following weeks and months you can derive great benefit by holding your totals between 35 and 45 miles. Because you will not be increasing mileage you can be creative in other ways. Enter races. Vary your pace. Vary the terrain: run in the park; run at the beach; run in the mountains—be creative and have a great time.

- Experiment with other forms of exercise in addition to your 40 miles per week: bike riding; swimming; weight training; yoga; walking and hiking; rock climbing; gymnastics; tumbling; fencing; volleyball; tennis—there's no end to the possibilities.

Training Log: 7-Day/4-Week Schedule

WEEK 1

	DAY 1	DAY 2	DAY 3	DAY 4	DAY 5	DAY 6	DAY 7	7 DAY TOTAL
Daily Mileage								
Comments								
Pulse	AM | PM	AM | PM	AM | PM	AM | PM	AM | PM	AM | PM	AM | PM	WEIGHT

WEEK 2

	DAY 1	DAY 2	DAY 3	DAY 4	DAY 5	DAY 6	DAY 7	7 DAY TOTAL
Daily Mileage								
Comments								
Pulse	AM | PM	AM | PM	AM | PM	AM | PM	AM | PM	AM | PM	AM | PM	WEIGHT

Training Log: 7-Day/4-Week Schedule

WEEK 3

	DAY 1	DAY 2	DAY 3	DAY 4	DAY 5	DAY 6	DAY 7	7 DAY TOTAL
Daily Mileage								
Comments								
Pulse	AM | PM	AM | PM	AM | PM	AM | PM	AM | PM	AM | PM	AM | PM	WEIGHT

WEEK 4

	DAY 1	DAY 2	DAY 3	DAY 4	DAY 5	DAY 6	DAY 7	7 DAY TOTAL
Daily Mileage								
Comments								
Pulse	AM | PM	AM | PM	AM | PM	AM | PM	AM | PM	AM | PM	AM | PM	WEIGHT

Holding Pattern

Now we dig in for the long haul to toughen our fiber, strengthen our will and fool our bodies into believing that running 40 miles per week is the natural order of things.

If you have advanced at a prudent rate, no faster than suggested in the schedules, perhaps more slowly, you have probably arrived with few setbacks. If enthusiasm has gotten the best of you, you probably suffered the ills that surely befall the imprudent athlete.

A few days ago I saw a female runner sitting at the sidelines with a painfully swollen lower leg. She was seeking advice from a *ranking trackman* on how to continue training. He advised her to "ice" the swelling, tape the shin and foot, take some aspirin and continue training.

After the *track star* had left, I asked the girl how she had been training. "Oh, I guess I run about six miles or a little more every afternoon."

"How fast?"

She looked at me kind of funny. "Why as fast I can, of course, and a couple times a week I play racketball."

"A couple times a week?"

"Maybe three or four, and sometimes on Sunday I play baseball after my run.

My mind boggled. Even though giving advice was a futile gesture, I suggested to her she get completely off the foot and do alternative exercises for at least two weeks. If she felt like it, I told her she could certainly "ice" the lower leg and foot to bring the swelling down and numb the ache. "Once swelling is completely gone," I suggested, "you could try alternating hot soaks and ice packs. No guarantee, but some trainers think this promotes healing, especially when it's a ligament problem." I also thought she should see a podiatrist, and said so.

The Perfect Marathon — Part I

She thanked me for my advice and looked longingly at the track. Experience tells me the young track addict will probably lay off for a day (or two at the most) then go back to painful training. A shorter while later she will come down with a stress fracture . . .that is if she hasn't one already.

Since we are at this level, Step Eight, it's safe to assume that even those who had physical set-backs are now cured and whole again! Is it safe to make that assumption? I hope so. If you do have any lingering discomforts, now is certainly the time to take care of them.

Difficulties that crop up even when you are training sensibly can often be traced to wearing improper or worn-over shoes; canted, irregular or sharply curved running areas; and physical imbalances such as a short leg, or feet that turn this-a-way and that.

Are you wearing for-real jogging shoes or merely look-alikes from some discount store? Do your jogging shoes fit correctly and are they the correct shoes for you? Out of the dozen or so fine brands and models on the market, there may be one that's just perfect for you . . .it's certainly true in my case.

Perhaps you have been wearing the same shoe for too long and the heels have worn over. It is very important to keep them built up correctly. (Use a glue gun!) If you can afford it, it's a good idea to have at least two pairs of jogging shoes so you can trade off every other day. This gives the resting pair a chance to dry out, and they'll last much longer. I have three pairs, so I only have to wear a given pair once in three days. I build up the wear points every couple of weeks so they never feel run-over. My shoes have never been resoled and they're in good shape after more than two years . . .what more can I say!

Another source of continuing low-level discomfort is a lot of training done on sharply crowned roads, hike and bike trails with uneven surfaces, and on tracks, especially those that are less than a quarter of a mile in circumference (tighter on curves).

Try changing your course and paying even more attention to your stretches, warm-ups and warm-downs.

If all this doesn't help, your body, especially from the hips on down, could be put together funny. The feet are a predominant source of trouble. A visit to your local running-oriented podiatrist may be in order.

Very few of us are arranged in first-class order. I, for example, may look to be in excellent shape, but I have a couple of fused vertebrae in my neck, a slightly low shoulder and high hip, an off-kilter backbone from carrying too many books for too long in the same arm, and a mushed lumbar disc. The back aches once in awhile, especially if I sit slumped over for too long; but other than that, I really haven't had any running-related problems since I began wearing the right shoes and training with the aid of my brain instead of my ego.

The reason I'm now emphasizing the need to clear up any nagging difficulties is because during this step and from now on, we are going to be stressing the body in new and better ways.

Our longest run to date has been about 70 minutes, a very good chunk of time, but only a fraction of what we are going to do in the future. A marathon can take anywhere from less than two hours and fifteen minutes (world class) to something over five hours. Obviously this is going to be different than our present 1:10:00 maximum.

As you begin to increase your long run you may at first experience surprising and pronounced cramps in your calves or hamstrings (the back of your upper leg). Providing your diet and liquid intake are up to par, these rare episodes should be considered a normal result of high-level training. Unfortunately however, these cramps often occur during the most intimate of occasions . . .perhaps you'll choose not to go on. I can sympathize with your concerns and this is probably the best place to discuss *Love and the Long Distance Runner*. No doubt you've read that "Distance Runners Last Longer," "Runners Make Better Lovers," "Joggers Do It On The Road," and on and on. Great press! But is it true? Wellll . . .do you actually expect me, a runner, to destroy the myth—if it is a myth? The truth is, while runners may do a better job than your average non-athlete, he (or she) probably doesn't do it as often as legend would have it. After all, distance training takes a lot of energy . . .and there are those surprising cramps I mentioned earlier.

If you now have a so-so to pretty good love life, expect it to get even better. If you already have a fantastic love life don't be surprised if the frequency comes down a little . . .but not the quality . . .and it's quality that counts . . .doesn't it.

Our long mileage day may be going up at too fast a rate for some of you, and this will be expecially true if you are training in hot or humid weather. There *are* a couple of things you can try to help get you over the hump. First, you can stretch the increases over a much longer period of time. The other approach, which I prefer, is to hold at a particular level for one or two extra weeks, then make the scheduled jump.

When you look at this month's chart, you will notice two changes. An extra day off has been added and the weekly total has been lowered.

The third day of each week is your speed day, and it is listed in miles (1½ - 2 - 2). All others are in minutes which can still be converted to miles by dividing by 9.

	Day 1	Day 2	Day 3	Day 4	Day 5	Day 6	Day 7	
Week One	75	off	35	(1½-2-2)	off	45	35	[+43, +43]=36miles
Week Two	80	off	35	(1¾-2-2)	off	45	35	[+40, +40]=36.3mi
Week Three	83	off	35	(2-2-2)	off	45	35	[+40, +40]=37-mi
Week Four	90	off	40	(2-2-2)	off	45	35	[+40, +40]×38¼mi

Please see Step Seven, page 65, for instructions on how to use the extra mileage (+) at the end of each week.

We end the final week with a time total of approximately 5:42 or 38 miles at an average pace of 9 minutes per mile. This is about 2 miles less than we totaled at the end of Step Seven but our long day has reached *10 miles*.

Think back when you were struggling to make your first nonstop one mile. That wasn't really so very long ago and look where you are now! You might also look again at that "before" picture. Earlier we talked about stringing 26.2 one mile runs together. Now all you have to string together is a little more than two and a half of your long runs. Isn't that something!

For months now I have been saying "slow down and save your breath," but as you get into the longer runs, going too fast will probably not be a concern for most of you. What may happen is you will tend to get into a groove: a set pace, mile after mile. Getting "in the groove" is not necessarily bad—the hypnotic effect of staying in pattern will help the long miles go by—however during training you should attempt to break out of the groove occasionally and speed up just a little bit for between a hundred yards and half a mile, then settle back into pace. At the end of the long run, as in all your training runs, speed up toward the end for a couple of hundred yards, then jog until your breathing is normal.

When you get into your fast day, use your first mile or mile and a half to fully warm-up, then either stop and stretch for a couple of minutes or go directly to the speed run. For the 2 miles of speed work, go into the run moderately faster than normal training and try to pick up speed gradually throughout the distance. Your last quarter should be the fastest quarter, and the last eighth should be the fastest part of the run . . . but still not quite all-out.

The schedule indicates a 2 mile warm-down jog after the speed work. If you can do more than 2 miles of jogging after the fast run, this would be a great place to use up a little of that bracketed time (+) shown at the end of each week.

When you started jogging you wanted to go fast, Fast, FAST, but I kept telling you to slow down and save your breath. Well, now you have paid some of your dues and you're going to get your chance to ZOOom.

Since you're training for yourself instead of against some arbitrary standard, a stopwatch is strictly optional for *most* of the fast stuff. Maybe every couple of weeks, or once a month, you may want to time yourself to see where you are in relation to where you were, but other than that, who needs it!

The fast miles will still be held to one day, but that day is going to have more miles. They won't be gut-wrenching miles, but they will be plenty fast enough to pose a challenge.

Step 8 Notes

- Up until now the purpose of these programs has been to lay down a training base and to help you achieve a healthy, active lifestyle . . . the lifestyle of a vibrant athlete. Your body should now be used to the stress of long miles and consistent training.

- Morning and evening limbering and stomach exercises should now be an integral part of your day.

- Within the framework of 35/45 miles per week, it is now time to make changes in the quality or intensity of the individual runs. Borrowing from your other days, gradually increase the length of one of your runs. Your week should have a long run, a run of moderate distance, and several shorter ones. As the weeks pass the long run gets longer, but the weekly total mileage remains more or less the same.

- Each week during this period should also have a day (a short day) when you run a bit faster than normal—but remember to fully warm-up first and allow enough slow jogging at the end for your breath to return to normal. During your other runs, including the long one, maintain a moderate overall pace, but within that framework include some brief periods of faster running always followed by a slowdown for recovery.

- Because this is a time of consistent weekly mileage, it is also a good time to concentrate a little more on weight-training, especially for the lower body.

Training Log: 7-Day/4-Week Schedule

WEEK 1

	DAY 1	DAY 2	DAY 3	DAY 4	DAY 5	DAY 6	DAY 7	7 DAY TOTAL
Daily Mileage								
Comments								
Pulse	AM PM	AM PM	AM PM	AM PM	AM PM	AM PM	AM PM	WEIGHT

WEEK 2

	DAY 1	DAY 2	DAY 3	DAY 4	DAY 5	DAY 6	DAY 7	7 DAY TOTAL
Daily Mileage								
Comments								
Pulse	AM PM	AM PM	AM PM	AM PM	AM PM	AM PM	AM PM	WEIGHT

Training Log: 7-Day/4-Week Schedule

WEEK 3

	DAY 1	DAY 2	DAY 3	DAY 4	DAY 5	DAY 6	DAY 7	7 DAY TOTAL
Daily Mileage								
Comments								
Pulse	AM	PM	AM	PM	AM	PM	AM	PM	AM	PM	AM	PM	AM	PM	WEIGHT

WEEK 4

	DAY 1	DAY 2	DAY 3	DAY 4	DAY 5	DAY 6	DAY 7	7 DAY TOTAL
Daily Mileage								
Comments								
Pulse	AM	PM	AM	PM	AM	PM	AM	PM	AM	PM	AM	PM	AM	PM	WEIGHT

A Marathon For Training

Are your friends, family and business associates beginning to get tired of your "war stories"? Are they getting bored with never-ending tales of new Personal Records, of newly discovered muscles or little aches and pains? Are they being driven slowly up the wall by accounts of your latest misadventures with packs of wild jogger-eating dogs, homicidal pickup trucks and urchins with water hoses? (Wet/cool bodies feel wonderful but squishy running shoes usually lead to blisters.)

No doubt some of your friends have taken up smoking an extra pack a day, or downing a few extra doughnuts in direct defiance of your hard-won good health and overpowering exuberance. To heck with them! I know there're people out there who appreciate what we're going through.

Around the time I was taking part in my first marathon, Janet (Ralph's wife) said that talking to me was like taking a trip in a *time machine*. Almost every word I said, every comment, observation, complaint and dumb new theory was a replay of what she had heard from Ralph 6 years before. "It's really great fun," she assured me, but then, she doesn't like to hurt anyone's feelings.

Mrs. Nolte is a very understanding woman. At the finish of the Crowley Marathon she was there waiting for me with four gigantic cups of iced Coke. Without saying a word she handed me the first, which I smoothly downed. She took the empty and handed me a full one, which I again smoothly downed. She didn't say a word during this ritual. When all four were gone she gave me her heart warming congratulations; but knowing the condition of my mind at the time, she wasn't expecting an immediate answer.

Ralph had finished about forty-five minutes before me, so he was in good shape to offer a critique on my race.

"Nice finish," he told me. "Very fast, lots of flash. Probably means you were taking it too

easy during the race...we did expect you to finish about 15 minutes sooner." No molly coddling from old Ralph as you can see.

Two hours later I was trotting up and down stairs while Ralph was having a little trouble just getting in and out of his car. "Just goes to prove," he mumbled, "you took it too easy during the race, mumble, mumble."

I write this in part as jest, but in essence it's true. When my buddy races he gives it his all, sometimes hanging right on the edge of disaster. When the system works, it really works. But when it fails it can result in serious injuries including muscle tears that can force a lay-off for months with additional months of slow rebuilding.

My style is to run well within my capabilities. While this may not be quite so devil-may-care or "competitive," it usually results in a challenging race, a strong finish and a quick recovery. As I get better I finish sooner, but still remain far from the edge of disaster.

As I run I keep check on my body. I press ahead a little harder to test the systems; hold there if possible, cut back if necessary.

Perhaps after a first marathon you'll find that this system works for you or perhaps you *damn the torpedoes* and opt for the possibility of tearing up your body once or twice a year. It's all up to you and your personality.

Perhaps it is still too soon to speak of such things. We haven't even begun to train for a marathon—much less run one. So back to basics: this month's schedule.

	Day 1	Day 2	Day 3	Day 4	Day 5	Day 6	Day 7	
Week One	90	off	45	(2-2½-2)	off	45	35	[+35, +40]=38.7mi
Week Two	99	0ff	45	(2-2½-2)	18	45	35	[+25, +32]=39.7mi
Week Three	99	off	45	(2-3-2)	18	45	35	[+25, +30]=40mi
Week Four	108	off	50	(2-3-2)	off	45	35	[+25, +28]=39.3mi

We are holding our mileage steady, finishing the week with a total of 39 miles. Our longest run was 12 miles, up from last week. Sounds great! But as fine as it sounds, we still haven't begun to train for a marathon...this has all been kid-stuff.

This is as far as we can go until you make the big decision: WHEN ARE YOU GOING TO RUN YOUR MARATHON? Need help? The best place to find marathon race schedules is in *Runner's World* magazine.

From this point in your training it takes approximately 3 months to get ready. Pick the race you want to enter. The date should be 14 weeks or more away from the day you finish Step Nine: Week Four. If it is further away than that, keep working on this step until the race gets closer, then go into marathon training with Step Ten.

If the race you want to enter is closer than 14 weeks, say 11 to 12 weeks away, you might get ready by trimming the next three steps a little. If the race is closer than 11 weeks away, let it pass.

By pushing yourself to the extreme it would be *possible* to get your weekly totals and long runs up to marathon level in six weeks, plus a pre-race pull-back and race week itself, for a total of eight weeks. However, you would be seriously risking injury and would be defeating the purpose of the book: to run The Perfect Marathon.

While you're deciding what to do, let's discuss this step's speed run. During these past four weeks your fast run has gone up from 2 miles to 3. Because we are running a total of 39 miles per week, our fast run is longer by one third than the 5% we are allowed...and this doesn't take into consideration the fast stuff we are doing during our regular runs. Therefore it's important that our fast runs be mostly aerobic.

After your warm-up run, pick up speed until you feel that any faster and you will begin to breathe hard, then cut back just a little. Whenever you get the warning that you are about to pass over into the anaerobic state (hard breathing), pull back. Continue to run right on the edge. As your system gets used to the exertion you may be able to speed up just a little, but cut back the second you feel a warning. Continue in this manner until you enter the last two hundred yards (about half a lap), then put on a little pressure.

As you move into the last 75 or 100 yards you should be going *almost* flat out. Run *past* your starting mark, then cut back to a dead-slow jog—don't stop. Continue slow jogging until your breathing is easy, then do the rest of your day's run at a normal pace. Finish with at least five minutes of stretches.

It's been a long time since I've mentioned the morning and evening stretches and sit-ups. I trust you're still doing them. Now that you're going faster and longer, your leg muscles are going to want

to tighten up, so these stretches in the morning and evening, and before and after every workout, are really important.

The fast run has been put out of the way, so perhaps I can help you with some thoughts on picking a marathon.

Some choose the race closest to their 25th, 30th, 35th, 40th, 45th, 50th (etc.) birthday. Others pick on the basis of the weather or the accessibility of the race site. Still others choose a race where they know there will be lots of friends watching and cheering…which brings to mind the title of this Step: *A Marathon for Training*.

One thing you cannot gain from training, reading or talking with your friends is experience…and there is nothing like the experience of actually running a marathon to slam home the points that never seemed too important on first hearing.

I knew about pacing before I ran my first marathon, but its monumental significance didn't come through until I was dragging and whimpering at 22 miles.

I had heard that it was a good idea to take water the first time it was offered, and to continue taking it throughout most of the race. But I wasn't thirsty at 2, 3, 5, and 7 miles so I didn't take water until later, and by then it was far too late.

Somewhere in my brain was the correct information, but it wasn't brought home until I learned from experience.

The most important thing I learned from experience was if you train properly and pace correctly, *THERE IS NO WALL!* That, I think, is one of the most satisfying bits of information I can pass on to you.

My advice then is for you to pick an out-of-town marathon which takes place at least 14 weeks from now, and which takes place about 5 weeks before your hometown marathon.

If you run the first marathon as a training run—well within your capabilities—the 26.2 miles will count as a *long 20 miler*. You will gain tremendous experience, you will have a week to *come down* from the race, two weeks to *peak* for the important one in front of your friends, a week to settle in, and voila, THE BIG RACE.

If this is impossible for you to arrange, trust in the experience of others, follow the *Marathon Preparation* that follows in Steps 10 through 12, and you will run The Perfect Marathon the first time out on someone else's experience and on YOUR SWEAT, GUTS, DETERMINATION AND TRAINING.

Step 9 Notes

- This step continues at the 35/45 miles per week level and can continue indefinitely . . . the longer the better.

- Don't neglect the morning and evening stretches and stomach exercises, they are as important now as they have ever been. In addition, if you haven't been doing any weight-training for the legs and upper body, now would be a good time to start.

- During this period of steadily maintained mileage you will be in a position to further experiment with running styles, situations and conditions.

- With a basic level of fitness achieved, speedwork will become a more important aspect of training and should closely *approach* the anaerobic state for brief periods, with always enough jogging to completely recover.

- Now is the time to even further increase the length of your longer run and moderate run by borrowing from other days.

- Depending upon how you feel, train from 4 to 6 days per week . . . be sure to take at least one day off per week, but try not to take off two days in a row.

The Perfect Marathon — Part I

Training Log: 7-Day/4-Week Schedule

WEEK 1

	DAY 1	DAY 2	DAY 3	DAY 4	DAY 5	DAY 6	DAY 7	7 DAY TOTAL
Daily Mileage								
Comments								
Pulse	AM | PM	AM | PM	AM | PM	AM | PM	AM | PM	AM | PM	AM | PM	WEIGHT

WEEK 2

	DAY 1	DAY 2	DAY 3	DAY 4	DAY 5	DAY 6	DAY 7	7 DAY TOTAL
Daily Mileage								
Comments								
Pulse	AM | PM	AM | PM	AM | PM	AM | PM	AM | PM	AM | PM	AM | PM	WEIGHT

Training Log: 7-Day/4-Week Schedule

WEEK 3

	DAY 1	DAY 2	DAY 3	DAY 4	DAY 5	DAY 6	DAY 7	7 DAY TOTAL
Daily Mileage								
Comments								
Pulse	AM PM	AM PM	AM PM	AM PM	AM PM	AM PM	AM PM	WEIGHT

WEEK 4

	DAY 1	DAY 2	DAY 3	DAY 4	DAY 5	DAY 6	DAY 7	7 DAY TOTAL.
Daily Mileage								
Comments								
Pulse	AM PM	AM PM	AM PM	AM PM	AM PM	AM PM	AM PM	WEIGHT

Beginning The Big Push

I don't remember where I first heard this, but when an old geezer was asked what it felt like to be 90, he answered, "I feel like a twenty year old but with something wrong with him."

I was swiftly approaching 40 when I decided to attempt a marathon. I felt I was in the best condition of my entire life and this would be a good way of proving it…at least to myself. I would go through a positive *rite of passage* rather than a negative one. I wasn't about to mope about reading those funny(?) geriatric greeting cards people get on their 40th birthday.

I realize that this may be a sign of mental pathology, but I've spent most of my important birthday years trying to prove that I am actually getting younger.

My 15th year was spent eating chocolate chip cookies, reading science fiction and getting fat. My 30th year was spent climbing mountains. My 40th year was to be *The Year of the Marathon.* Is this to be *YOUR YEAR OF THE MARATHON?*

If you are ready to begin Step Ten, it means you've made the "Big Decision," and have your sights set on a very particular race. If you have not chosen the marathon date, read on but until you choose an *exact date,* continue with variations on Steps Eight and Nine. There is a reason.

In order to do your best in a major event such as the marathon, it is important to plan your training so that you "peak" at a certain time. By "peaking" we mean reaching an optimum physical and emotional level.

If you "peak" too soon, you may be forced to continue an ultra-high level of training for too long, and when the race date finally arrives you may be physically worn out, in a state of depression and wondering why you ever got into marathons in the first place.

By using the peaking process in a creative manner, you can run several marathons in a short period of time, and be at or near your peak for each. In fact, if you use this system, a marathon can become a stepping stone to swiftly improving performance.

When you are running two marathons in a two-month period, you can reach a level of fitness and excitement, burn off some energy with the first marathon, retrench for a week, strive for a new and higher peak, go all-out in the second race, and then go into a fairly long-term low-level rest and training period to recover.

I've used this "domino" system with three consecutive marathons in three months, cutting my time by about 20 minutes in each of the second two races. This, however, finished me for the rest of the season. I attempted to get back into training several times, but it was futile. *I* was really burnt out...not my body so much, but my brain.

This is how that year looked: six months of training followed by three months of marathoning, which I experienced in the most euphoric/hypnotic state you can possibly imagine—high in the clouds the entire time. Next came three months of recuperation—mostly mental—and some very light sporadic training. Then, of course, the cycle began again.

ONWARD TO STEP TEN. For this step we will be switching *from charts with times to charts with miles*. It is perfectly all right to continue to run on the basis of time, but it is also important to control the mileage.

Until now we have been *assuming* that you can run at an average pace of 9 minutes per mile. Some of you may actually be running closer to a 10 minute pace, while others are probably running eights or better.

The 10 minute people should be trying to get their time down bit by bit, while remaining within the pulse range of 120-150. You still have almost three months to get it down.

While it is certainly possible to run a marathon at a 10 minute or slower pace, 4½ hours is a very long time to be out there. REMEMBER, *every 10 seconds you can trim* off your training miles now—providing you remain aerobic—may get you to the marathon finish line as much as 4½ minutes sooner without any extra strain.

Those of you who are able to run aerobically at an 8 minute per mile pace, congratulations. You're right where you should be. Don't go any faster (except for spurts and finishes) during your regular training. During your long run go slower.

The Perfect Marathon — Part I

A note to all regardless of training speed: as you work your way through this step, try to curb your enthusiasm and don't exceed the distances given for the long runs—too often.

There will be times when you're out on the course doing a planned long run (or even a short one) when you'll feel fantastic—as if you could run forever. At times like these it is a fine idea to let your shortest run become the week's long one. If this feeling comes over you while the scheduled long run is in progress, I won't *tell* you not to go further—you'll have to let your body be your guide—but be sure and subtract the extra mileage from your next regular run.

While I suggest not going overboard on the long runs, it is also important that you don't come out short on your weekly totals. It is also important that you continue to include at least one rest day, or very short day, so you don't exhaust yourself.

Since we all differ so greatly in natural ability, inclination and freedom to train, *beginning this month there will be three charts* and three different preparation programs for the marathon.

The first chart (A) offers a basic program that can get you across the finish in reasonable comfort providing you are scrupulous in your training and preparation, and providing you are extremely realistic in setting your time goal and sticking to a predetermined pace.

The second chart (B) will, if given half a chance, enable you to run *The Perfect Marathon*.

The third chart (C) is a mind and body boggler. Personally I wouldn't even attempt it…my body begins to break down much beyond 65 miles per week. However, I know many runners who thrive on 75 to 150 miles per week.

If you are daft enought to begin with Schedule C, remember you can always switch back to B—if you're not injured—or stop your progression on the chart and hold at that point until just before the race.

BASIC SCHEDULE A

	Day 1	Day 2	Day 3	Day 4	Day 5	Day 6	Day 7	
Week One	12	off	6	(2-3-2)	off	6	5	[+4]Total=40 miles
Week Two	13	0ff	7	(2-3½-2)	off	6	5	[+3½]Total=42
Week Three	14	off	7	(2-3½-2)	off	6½	5	[+0]Total=40
Week Four	12	2	7	(2-4-2)	off	7	5	[+3]Total=44

BASIC SCHEDULE B

	Day 1	Day 2	Day 3	Day 4	Day 5	Day 6	Day 7	
Week One	12	off	7	(2-3-2)	off	7	5	[+2]Total=40 miles
Week Two	13	2	7½	(2-3½-2)	off	7½	5½	[+2]Total=45
Week Three	14	off	7½	(2-3-2)	off	7½	5	[+0]Total=41
Week Four	13	2	8	(2-4-2)	off	8	5	[+1]Total=45

SCHEDULE C: VERY HEAVY, NOT FOR FIRST-TIME MARATHONERS

	Day 1	Day 2	Day 3	Day 4	Day 5	Day 6	Day 7	
Week One	13¼	off	6	(2-3-2)	off	7	5	[+4¾]Total=43 mi
Week Two	14½	off	6½	(2-3-2)	off	6½	5½	[+7]Total=47
Week Three	16	2	7	(2-3½-2)	off	7½	6	[+4]Total=50
Week Four	17½	2½	7	(2-3½-2)	off	7½	6½	[+4½]Total=53

Well there you are, three different strokes for three different groups of folks. From these you should be able to adapt a Step 10 to suit your own needs and abilities.

Each week on the chart is seven days long, naturally, but I don't designate the actual days … though on my personal chart the first day is always Sunday. You don't have to begin the week on a Sunday, but I find that doing so makes planning for the race much easier.

The final week before a marathon begins with a moderately long run, carbohydrate depletion, carbohydrate loading, tapering off of training and THE MARATHON. Because the process takes six days and races are usually on Saturday, I think it's a good idea to get used to doing your long run on the weekend.

Regardless of where you start your week, the long run is to be slow and broken from time to time for water and other pit stops. One of the main reasons for the extra long run is to get used to being on the road for extended periods. Stopping for a minute or two to get water actually extends your training time, and while we won't approach marathon distance during training because we are running slower, we *will* approach the marathon *time*.

These increasingly long runs, coupled with the fast ones, are going to tie up your legs if you aren't careful. Stretching and warming-up were important earlier but are doubly important now …especially before and after the fast ones.

Speed days are divided into a medium length warm-up run, a speed run almost *at the limits of your aerobic capability* (any faster and you'd be breathing hard) coupled with an ⅛ mile fast finish. All this is followed by a medium length warm-down as long *or longer than indicated in the schedule*.

The rest of the runs for the week can be taken as shown or split into two or more runs. I would strongly advise having at least two split days in a week. Use the extra miles (those in brackets) as you will, but use them.

Run the daily at speeds between 8 minutes per mile and 9:15 per mile if you are able, but be sure not to let yourself get out of breath for more than a minute or so at a time, and then only slightly. Always jog long enough to get your breathing back to normal.

I think you're going to find that one of the great limiting factors in training for distance is the ability of your limbs, joints and feet to withstand the incessant pounding. If you can find practical ways of adding non-running cardiovascular exercises to your routine, you will be way ahead of the game. There are many possibilities. For example, if you live 5 or 10 miles from school or your place of work, and ride a bike there and back every day at a brisk pace, you will enhance your training. If you wish to substitute rather than add, figure that 30 minutes of brisk bike riding can replace 2½ miles of slow jogging. If the biking is nonstop, it will replace 3 miles of jogging…but don't use it to replace any of your long run or fast run.

If you swim a lot, figure that as an added benefit, but don't use swimming as a replacement for jogging on the Marathon Preparation Schedule.

Your weight is almost as important as your training. If you begin now to slowly whittle away at the ounces, the pounds will disappear as the training mileage goes up.

The Perfect Marathon — Part I

My approach to weight control is simple and I cover diet later on. Basically, I eat citrus fruits (grapefruit), some protein and a little carbohydrate (wheat germ) for breakfast. Breakfast is a must. I start other meals with a large green salad without oil. Fats and oils of any kind will put on blubber faster than anything—blubber to blubber. Eat little or no sugar or any foods with added sugar (including honey), and exercise instead of having a coffee break—maybe even instead of lunch. Other than that you can pretty much eat what you want. Simply put, added fats and sugar screw you up, green salads fill you up, and jogging trims you down.

Some runners make a big deal out of using racing shoes that cut an ounce or two off their running weight, yet they eat a kilo of spaghetti a day the week before the race. It's a far, far better thing to take five pounds off your gut than to worry about two ounces on your feet.

Step 10 Notes

- This is the first period of actual marathon training. Successfully running and completing the marathon requires a well integrated body and mind. The Greeks were right, it is best to be totally fit.

- Peripheral exercises such as: sit-ups; leg curls and extensions; resistance movements for the arms, chest and back; and stretches and limbering are now nearly as important as the road mileage and speed work.

- Body weight is extremely important . . . low body weight that is. Excess poundage unduly stresses the joints and ligaments, while every blob of fat lost makes running easier and allows you to go further and faster without added effort. Perhaps it sounds a bit Einsteinian, but one of the secrets of *The Perfect Marathon* is conservation of energy: low body weight; economical running style; even pace.

- While your pace during the marathon should be even, it should also be as brisk as you can manage it. There is no sense in spending 5 hours on the course if you are capable of finishing in four and a half hours, four hours or faster. During this step's training runs try and pick up the average pace just a little. You will probably discover that you have settled into a groove and are actually already capable of cutting seconds off your mile time.

- Going fast may not be your goal, but every 30 seconds cut from your mile during the marathon means you will be able to enjoy your beer or Coke about 13 minutes sooner . . . worth thinking about. The sooner you finish, the sooner you can glory in your accomplishment.

Training Log: 7-Day/4-Week Schedule

WEEK 1

	DAY 1	DAY 2	DAY 3	DAY 4	DAY 5	DAY 6	DAY 7	7 DAY TOTAL
Daily Mileage								
Comments								
Pulse	AM | PM	AM | PM	AM | PM	AM | PM	AM | PM	AM | PM	AM | PM	WEIGHT

WEEK 2

	DAY 1	DAY 2	DAY 3	DAY 4	DAY 5	DAY 6	DAY 7	7 DAY TOTAL
Daily Mileage								
Comments								
Pulse	AM | PM	AM | PM	AM | PM	AM | PM	AM | PM	AM | PM	AM | PM	WEIGHT

Training Log: 7-Day/4-Week Schedule

WEEK 3

	DAY 1		DAY 2		DAY 3		DAY 4		DAY 5		DAY 6		DAY 7		7 DAY TOTAL
Daily Mileage															
Comments															
	AM	PM	AM	PM	AM	PM	AM	PM	AM	PM	AM	PM	AM	PM	WEIGHT
Pulse															

WEEK 4

	DAY 1		DAY 2		DAY 3		DAY 4		DAY 5		DAY 6		DAY 7		7 DAY TOTAL
Daily Mileage															
Comments															
	AM	PM	AM	PM	AM	PM	AM	PM	AM	PM	AM	PM	AM	PM	WEIGHT
Pulse															

Piling It Higher, Deeper and Faster

It's getting so close I can practically smell the liniment and hear the tears of joy and frustration splashing on the pavement.

Although our mileage is getting longer and our fast runs are getting faster, in many ways the training should be easier. We have a fixed and monumental goal only a short time away. We no longer have to think in terms of many months or years of slow methodical building—of week after week of 2 and 3 mile runs to build up a base. We now have the base and are making the final rush towards THE PERFECT MARATHON.

During the final weeks before my first marathon I was in a naturally induced altered state of consciousness almost twenty-four hours a day. I really can't say how I appeared to others, my training partners and their families, but I felt as if I were being propelled by some otherworldly power.

On my nightly "solo" runs I was accompanied by gods that lofted me with their powerful wings and carried me with the gentle force of the wind across the finish line.

As the days went on, I came to be on such good terms with these gods that when one would prepare to loft me down the last 200 yards, I'd look up over my shoulder and whisper "not yet, not yet," and I would pick up speed and power down the stretch on my own. Fifty yards from the finish I'd look up over my shoulder again and whisper "now." The great wings would scoop down behind me, my feet would lose contact with the track, and I'd soar effortlessly across the finish and beyond.

During this period I think it is important to be around people who are training for or are excited about the upcoming marathon. To experience the real joy of final preparation and the event itself, you should share it with others as well as cherish it inside. Stay away from folks who tend to rain on your parade.

The Perfect Marathon — Part I

By this point in my training, almost all my friends were either marathoners, prospective marathoners, runners or serious joggers, so I had little difficulty finding support and emotional sharing. Even my parents, a couple of thousand miles away, were sharing the experience and participating by clipping and sending articles on running from their local newspaper.

In my letters to friends and relatives I casually mentioned that I was training for a marathon. Even though most of them weren't exactly sure what a marathon was, they knew it was *A Big Deal* and were duly impressed. Their notes of interest, encouragement, and occasionally, awe, arrived just when I needed them most, and added immeasurably to my growing euphoria.

As you are taken up by the euphoria, you will begin to feel invincible. In many ways you will be, but there is a danger of losing contact with your body. Twinges in the foot, awareness of the knee, something funny about your calf or maybe just the slightest tenderness when you squeeze your Achilles tendon: these are warnings that your new increases in mileage or speed may be just a little too much.

You probably noticed that in the last set of charts our long run and total mileage did not get progressively longer. Instead, mileage advanced, regressed, advanced, etc. The idea is to push the body to new heights and then give it a chance to rest before going on to even greater heights.

The Schedule C, which is definitely not recommended for inexperienced marathoners, makes regular advances without retrenching. The rationale is that experienced runners have a long-maintained base on which to build. And they have already been at the 50 - 60 - 70 mile per week, and 20 mile long run level, many times before. They are not really reaching for great new heights but are visiting past glories and advancing slightly to a new plateau.

Beware. If you attempt Schedule C without a long-term training background, you may put yourself out of commission for a long time. Better to err on the side of conservatism and save your all-out effort for the second or third race...or there may not be a first one.

Regardless of whether you use charts A, B, or C, all have something in common during the second week. In the place reserved for the speed day you will see (½ - 5mi TT - ½). That is the day for the first *Time Trial*. The first number refers to a minimum of one half mile of slow jogging to warm-up in addition to your usual stretching and limbering. The final figure refers to a minimum of one-half mile of slow jogging to warm-down followed by stretching. If you are able to do more than a half-mile at the end of the Time Trial, do so.

The 5mi TT is a five mile run as fast as you can go. Pick a comfortable time of day to run and be sure you haven't had anything to eat for at least two hours. Your clothes should be comfortable, shoes fitting correctly and socks unbunched.

If possible have one or more friends run with you…preferably runners who are a little faster than you. Another possibility is to have someone pace you for the first 2½ miles and a second runner pace you for the remaining 2½ miles.

During the run you should either carry a stopwatch to monitor your pace at quarter mile intervals and to get an exact finish time, or you should have someone at the side of the track calling out quarter mile times and recording your final time.

During the Time Trial you will have to be very careful not to burn yourself out by the second or third mile. Your pace should be more or less even, but there may be enough left at the end for you to give it a real go for the money over the last hundred yards.

You'll probably be a gasping wreck for a few minutes after the Time Trial, but try to keep going a slow jog for at least a few yards, then continue walking and jogging for at least a half mile or until you feel you're back to normal. Did you or your friend remember to record the exact finish time? You don't want to have to go through a run like that again.

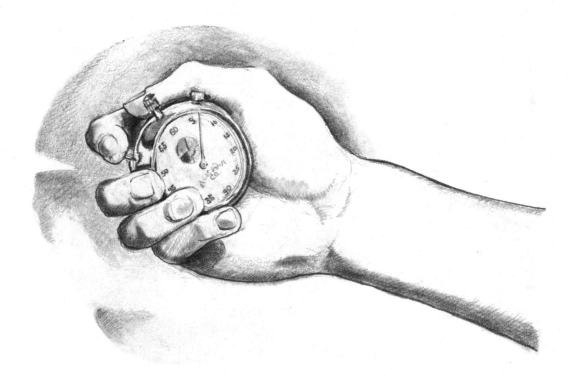

Now what do we have besides tired legs, an aching chest and a number? We have the first *magic key* to the marathon.

Elsewhere in the book you will find a miracle of modern research: The fantastic *Jim Dandy - Double Superheterodyne - Magnificent Magic - Marathon Predictor*. This amazing instrument has many uses. In this step we will only scratch the surface.

Turn to the Marathon Predictor Chart on page 178 and run your finger down the left hand column until you find your time for the 5 miles. If your time isn't listed, pick the next slower. Look across to the fourth column of figures—the number in parentheses. Note down that number. For example, if your 5 mile time was 35 minutes and 11 seconds (35:11), look down the left hand column and you'll find 35:00, and 35:15. Your exact number isn't listed, but 35:15 is the next slower, so that's the one to use.

From 35:15 go across to the fourth column and you will find (7:45). If your 5 mile time had been 36:30, you'd find eight minutes one second (8:01) in the fourth column. The number in brackets in the fourth column is your minimum one mile pace for all speed runs between now and the marathon.

The Perfect Marathon — Part I

Maintain this pace evenly throughout the speed run, but finish with a somewhat faster spurt over the final hundred yards or so, then continue to jog for a half mile longer.

During the speed runs you should carry a stopwatch to monitor your pace. If you are trying to maintain an 8 minute pace, you should come around each quarter in two minutes. Once you get used to it, you can learn to maintain a pace within a second or two of the selected time.

A way to make the timekeeping simple is to figure on the basis of 2 minutes. If you come around in 2 you are going at an 8 minute pace. If you come around 5 seconds beyond 2 minutes the first time you are going at an 8:20 pace (5 seconds x 4 = 20 seconds.) If the second hand continues to advance 5 more seconds each quarter you know you are holding the 8:20 pace.

If the second hand is retarded 5 seconds at the end of a quarter you are at a 7:40 pace, and if it continues to retard 5 more seconds each quarter you are right on 7:40.

If you are going a little slower than 8 minutes per mile, and the second hand is just before straight up when you *complete a mile,* you know you are just so many seconds before 9 minutes.

Standing still you wouldn't need a system like this. When you are running it is often difficult to read the numbers, but you can see the relative position of the second hand.

I have been assuming that you use a regular windup stopwatch with hands. Wrist chronometers with digital readouts are sometimes easier on the benumbed minds, and a few will give you both splits and total time with no calculations necessary on your part. At the time of this writing, it is possible to buy stop watches for from fifteen dollars to fifteen thousand dollars. At first an inexpensive hand held job available at the local drugstore will work just fine. Later you may want to get a wrist chronometer. They can be purchased at running shops and discount stores. Because models and prices change so often, I hesitate to mention brand names, but this much I *can* say: stay away from watches that are plated. They should either be made from stainless steel or plastic, and they should be waterproof. The first wrist chronometer I used for running corroded inside and out in just a few months. It was goldplated and not, I sadly found out, waterproof...a hundred bucks down the drain. My present chronometer cost thirty-five dollars, is made out of plastic, works perfectly and after a year of hard use still looks new. It is easy to read in bright sun and has a little night-light for reading in the dark.

I think modern watches are fantastic, but they have one *BIG* drawback when you first begin to use them. They have so many buttons and functions that it is sometimes possible, in a fit of excitement, to push the wrong button and erase the entire program before you have a chance to see your time.

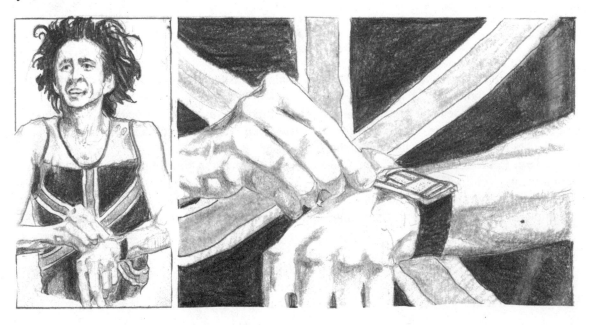

A friend of mine has a different problem. He has one of those $300 chronometers that rocket ship pilots and secret agents wear. At every marathon he clicks the watch into GO at the sound of the starter's gun and he's off. At the end of the race he's too excited to stop the watch and by the time he remembers, the $300 Wonder tells him the marathon took 12 hours and 7 seconds. At that rate he'll never break 3 hours…and we won't either unless we get back into training.

In these charts 5TT refers to the 5 mile Time Trial. In the weeks following the Time Trial your fast run should be whipped out at our new magic pace drawn from the Predictor Chart.

BASIC SCHEDULE A

	Day 1	Day 2	Day 3	Day 4	Day 5	Day 6	Day 7	
Week One	14	0ff	7½	(2-4-2)	2	7½	3	[+0]Total=42 miles
Week Two	15	0ff	8	(½-5TT-½)	off	8	5	[+2]Total=46
Week Three	13	2	7	(2-4-2)	off	7½	5½	[+1]Total=44
Week Four	15	off	8½	(2-4-2)	3	8	6	[+0]Total=48

SCHEDULE B

	Day 1	Day 2	Day 3	Day 4	Day 5	Day 6	Day 7	
Week One	14½	2	8¼	(2-4-2)	off	8½	5½	[+3½]Total=50 mi
Week Two	15	off	8½	(½-5TT-½)	off	8½	5	[+2]Total=45
Week Three	16	off	9	(2-4-2)	off	9	6	[+2]Total=50
Week Four	15	off	9½	(2-4-2)	2	9½	6½	[+4½]Total=55

SCHEDULE C: VERY HEAVY, NOT FOR FIRST-TIME MARATHONERS

	Day 1	Day 2	Day 3	Day 4	Day 5	Day 6	Day 7	
Week One	18	2¾	7½	(2-4-2)	2	8½	7	[+3¼]Total=57 mi
Week Two	18	3	8	(½-5TT-½)	2	9	7	[+4]Total=57
Week Three	18½	3¼	8¾	(2-4-2)	2	10	7½	[+2]Total=60
Week Four	19	3½	10	(2-5-1)	2¼	11	8¼	[+0]Total=62

The extra miles (+) are to be added to any run you like, except the long run and the fast run. Regular runs may be added together, divided and split in any way you like. I encourage you to use split-days *at least* twice a week. A split day can consist of two *or more* runs, 5 or more hours apart, in a single day. You might, for instance, run at 6 a.m., noon and again at 7:30 p.m. Every week should have at least one rest day or very short day.

As you finish this step your first marathon should be a faint glow six weeks down the road. If you've miscalculated or just gotten ahead of yourself, there's nothing to worry about.

If the race is actually seven weeks ahead instead of six, you have time for a breather…a rest week. The rest week will be the same for all three schedules.

ALTERNATE REST WEEK A, B, C: Step Eleven (if marathon is 7 weeks away.)
Week Five   off - 10 - 3 - (½ - 5 - ½) - 2 - 8 - off (+0) Total=29 miles

If, when you finish Step Eleven: Week Four, the marathon is only 5 weeks away instead of 6, you can still remain on schedule by eliminating Week One of Step Twelve, that is, begin Step Twelve with the second week.

The Perfect Marathon — Part I

From now on you should have no trouble with your training. You are in fantastic shape just rolling along; nothing short of a tornado or a supernova can stop you now. Excitement is building.

The training schedule will give you the results you need, but there is one important variable that will make the race even more enjoyable. I've mentioned it before, but since we are nearing the wire, it is important to cover it once more.

One of the three or four most important factors governing a successful marathon is weight. Up to a point, every ½ pound of fat you trim off your butt or gut will cut minutes off your marathon time, with no extra strain on your system. If you're not interested in coming in faster, I can put it another way. Taking off useless weight will make the marathon experience easier and far more enjoyable.

We have a trade-off here. Attempting to lose weight may make you weaker for a time and that could make training more difficult. Therefore, if you're going to lose weight it must be now, not just before the race. A happy note: once you get your body into the process of fat shedding, the extra training will keep it coming off.

How do you know if you need to lose? Aw come on now! You know! If you can grab a big pinch of fat at your waist, that's a good indication. Another way to look at weight is that if you look fairly normal and trim, with not much fat to pinch, figure you are about five to ten percent above optimum running weight.

The marathoner should have a *lean and hungry look*. George Sheehan, well known in running circles, says when friends tell him he *looks healthy*, he know's he's pounds overweight.

In order to avoid (as much as possible) a feeling of weakness while dieting, start your days with a high protein, low fat, moderate carbohydrate breakfast and include some citrus fruit such as grapefruit.

During the diet your bread should be whole wheat. *Natural* unflavored yogurt such as Dannon is a good food and a good snack food during this period. I first became aware of Dannon when they began to co-sponsor races and give out yogurt at Fun Runs and marathons. It *is* natural because I use it as a starter when I make homemade yogurt. Homemade yogurt, by the way, is a good deal less expensive than the commercial varieties, but it's less convenient.

Yogurt is easy to digest even for some people who can't tolerate milk, and if taken a spoonful at a time throughout the day it can help keep your blood sugar level up and allay feelings of hunger.

Dehydration during heavy summer training can be a serious problem, so dieting or not, drink plenty of water. Given the lousy condition of many municipal water supplies you may consider using bottled distilled water or a naturally effervescent bottled mineral water. *Perrier* mineral water also sponsors distance races. You can get their schedule of events by writing Great Waters of France, Inc., 950 3rd Ave., NY, NY 10022.

If you've been successful in cutting back on junk food over the past few months, chances are only a few days on a strict diet will get your body into the *weight reduction mood*.

Last year after dropping down to a plateau of 172 pounds I started losing weight so regularly that I had to up my intake of carbohydrates (wheat germ and whole wheat bread) to keep my weight from going below 160 . . . not that I wouldn't have been a faster runner at 155, but at 160 my running shorts were already beginning to slip off, and my slacks had a great folding overlap in them when I cinched my belt.

The point is, weight loss at this stage need not be an overly traumatic affair. A little rearranging of the diet and weight will come off of its own accord.

Here is a little scenario of my own weight history as it relates to running. Usually about 4 months before a marathon I start figuring it's time to *think* about upping my training. This produces a low level anxiety and a high level of avoidance behavior . . . which means I begin to eat junk food. I put down several fried pies for breakfast and a couple of poorboy sandwiches with french fries for lunch, and a ½ gallon of ice cream throughout the day. Now, I think ice cream is a fantastic food . . . in ½ pints. But in gallons and ½ gallons it's junk of the worst kind.

For dinner I usually have a large salad plus *lots* of other good stuff and finish off the ice cream. My weight begins to creep up. At this point I increase my training load and the weight gain levels off. I am now 10 pounds over my maximum running weight.

I cut back a little on junk, my weight begins to come down. If it is very hot and humid, I drink a couple of beers after every run. I stop losing weight. I am now only 8 pounds too heavy.

Two months and a week or so to the race, I completely cut out fried pies and poorboys. I am now only 6 pounds over maximum running weight. My weekly total mileage is swiftly rising and my long run is slowly but surely getting longer.

Ice cream is now a special treat reserved to one pint after my weekly speed run. Ralph and I arrange to finish our run at the local Baskin Robbins, where we sit, each nursing a pint...he with some flavor sweet enough to make your teeth tingle, me with a mixture of Mandarin-Chocolate Sherbet and Apricot-Brandy Yogurt. We eat slowly, knowing there's no second pint for the likes of us...but we glory in the fact that the night after the marathon we can *pig out*.

I am now about four pounds over what I consider maximum racing weight. Mileage continues to climb and the weight starts to come off too fast. I add a couple of slices of homemade whole wheat bread to my diet to keep my strength up and to slow the dropping poundage.

I've leveled off two pounds too heavy. Will I have to resort to the Marathoner's One Week Diet? I come back from a slow 20 mile run in 90° heat and high humidity. I've had two beers, a bottle of mineral water and a Coke. I stopped for water 5 times during the 20 mile run. Even after all that intake, I find that I'm 5 pounds underweight due to fluid loss.

I drink what seems like gallons of water the rest of the day and that evening I have a rich soup for dinner. In the morning, after ablutions, I weigh myself. I'm right at my target weight and there's still a couple of weeks to go.

During the next week and a half I lose a pound or two in preparation for carbohydrate loading. Race morning I'm a half pound lighter than maximum target weight…just perfect and I really didn't have to resort to a ''diet.''

My maximum target weight is 165. By what super-scientific method did I arrive at 165? At 165 I look thin and wiry and feel great. At 160 I look like a shell, feel weak and all my clothes fall off. I opted for 165. Is that scientific enough for you!

The fancy way to arrive at your target weight requires lab tests; measurements for percentage of body fat. Men should be under 15% and women under 20%. Top ranking male runners will be 6% fat, or less, while top female marathoners will be 12% body fat or less.

Even though low body weight is an unqualified boon to running (just look at 86 pound marathoner Miki Gorman), it does have at least one serious drawback. With all your posterior padding gone, you are going to find it extremely difficult to sit all the way through the awards banquet.

Step 11 Notes

- This is the second period of concentrated marathon training, and the program has been divided into three levels of intensity: ''A'' Basic; ''B'' Moderate; ''C'' Heavy.

- ''A'' is for those who have been forced (for whatever reason) to cut corners, or who have opted for a less intense level of preparation. ''B'' is for those who have followed the months of training programs fairly closely, and is the level most recommended. ''C'' is for experienced runners who have been training at least two years and who have run at least one previous marathon.

- This step, all three levels, has been designed for those who have picked a specific marathon and are working towards a particular date. However, even greater benefit will be derived if this level is maintained for an extra month—more or less.

Training Log: 7-Day/4-Week Schedule

WEEK 1

	DAY 1		DAY 2		DAY 3		DAY 4		DAY 5		DAY 6		DAY 7		7 DAY TOTAL
Daily Mileage															
Comments															
	AM	PM	AM	PM	AM	PM	AM	PM	AM	PM	AM	PM	AM	PM	WEIGHT
Pulse															

WEEK 2

	DAY 1		DAY 2		DAY 3		DAY 4		DAY 5		DAY 6		DAY 7		7 DAY TOTAL
Daily Mileage															
Comments															
	AM	PM	AM	PM	AM	PM	AM	PM	AM	PM	AM	PM	AM	PM	WEIGHT
Pulse															

Training Log: 7-Day/4-Week Schedule

WEEK 3

	DAY 1	DAY 2	DAY 3	DAY 4	DAY 5	DAY 6	DAY 7	7 DAY TOTAL
Daily Mileage								
Comments								
	AM | PM	AM | PM	AM | PM	AM | PM	AM | PM	AM | PM	AM | PM	WEIGHT
Pulse								

WEEK 4

	DAY 1	DAY 2	DAY 3	DAY 4	DAY 5	DAY 6	DAY 7	7 DAY TOTAL
Daily Mileage								
Comments								
	AM | PM	AM | PM	AM | PM	AM | PM	AM | PM	AM | PM	AM | PM	WEIGHT
Pulse								

Training Log: 7-Day/4-Week Schedule

WEEK 5 (ALTERNATIVE REST WEEK)

	DAY 1		DAY 2		DAY 3		DAY 4		DAY 5		DAY 6		DAY 7		7 DAY TOTAL
	AM	PM	AM	PM	AM	PM	AM	PM	AM	PM	AM	PM	AM	PM	
Daily Mileage															
Comments															
Pulse															WEIGHT

STEP TWELVE

The Time Has Come

Only six more weeks to go. It's hard to believe we have come so far. A few months ago many of us were sedentary slouches schlooming resignedly into middle age . . . and those were the 20-year-olds. Others were tired, office-bound 50-year-olds with aching backs, sloppy paunches and an eye on retirement. A great many were occasional joggers questing for broader horizons. Some were healthy "youngsters" tired of having the "old folks" continually lapping them at the track or easily passing them on the hike and bike trails.

Now is the time to get your *before* picture and then look at yourself in the mirror. Is that mirror image really you? You're darn right it is. Not only is it really you, but it is *The Real You!*

That real you is in better physical condition than almost everyone else in the world. Don't be misled by statistics. The National Jogging Association has been claiming there are 10 million joggers in the U.S.A. I have a bumpersticker that states "12 Million Joggers Can't Be Wrong." Others claim there are 25 million joggers in the U.S. To get anything like 25 million joggers, you'd need to count everyone who ever walked to the store to get a loaf of bread and every weekend golfer who was caught once without a golf cart. The lower 10 million and 12 million figures even count the occasional jogger, who may already have dropped out by the time the numbers are published. As some joggers drop out, however, others will jog up to take their place.

Out of the thousands of people who are jumping on the jogging bandwagon, only a small percentage are actually sticking it out long enough to get into really good shape. Out of these an even smaller number *considers* training for a marathon.

Be that as it may, the number of people who actually take part in the marathon is growing. Marathons that had 20 entries 5 years ago now often have a thousand, fifteen hundred and more.

In most marathons, approximately 25 to 30% drop out, usually after making it to the ten-mile mark and beyond...a good performance in anyone's book. I don't have any statistics to back this up, but I suspect that a large number of runners who drop out between 10 and 20 miles later come back to finish a marathon in good form. Not one of my running friends finished the first. Note: they finished *walking*. Some attempted two or three before finally running the entire distance. Since then they've all gone on to finish dozens in good form.

In every case they attributed their early dropout rate to defective training: total weekly mileage peaking at 25 to 35, long runs of only 8 to 10 miles…and not enough of these. One friend had a lifetime total of a little over 30 miles when he tried his first marathon.

Go back to the mirror and look at yourself again. You are not only among the physical elite but you are elite among the elite. You are now probably better trained than the vast majority of first time marathoners. With that in mind we tackle our *Big Step*.

The base is laid. Our hearts and circulatory systems are in top condition and the fat is melting off our bodies. Our sinews are like iron, and our lungs are tireless bellows. We'd rather run than eat and cocktail parties are a boring, vague memory from the past. Our conversation is almost entirely devoted to training and most of it takes place on the run. We have become monomaniacs but not social recluses, for our closest friends share the same monomania.

Where we used to read books on running as an excuse not to run, we now skim swiftly to get the essential points, anxious to be on the road applying them. So let's get the schedules down and get back on the road.

The second week of this step will be another Time Trial of 5 miles (5TT). Do the Time Trial the same way you did it in Step Eleven - carefully recording your finish time. This TT figure is one of the most important ingredients in achieving *The Perfect Marathon*.

This Step's schedule includes five weeks instead of four.

Notice the extra miles in brackets [+] for some weeks; other weeks, there are none. Regardless of whether or not you run extra miles, you should still be taking advantage of split days. The third and sixth days on these charts are particularly long and make ideal candidates for split routines.

Day Three: Week Four of the B Schedule is a 12-mile day. This could be split into 3-mile jogs in the morning and at lunch, and a 6-mile job in the evening.

The Perfect Marathon — Part I

BASIC SCHEDULE A

	Day 1	Day 2	Day 3	Day 4	Day 5	Day 6	Day 7	
Week One	14	off	9	(2-4-2)	3	8	4	[+0]Total=46 miles
Week Two	15	2	10	(1-5TT-1)	4	9	3	[+0]Total=50
Week Three	18	off	11	(2-4-2)	4	9	3	[+0]Total=52
Week Four	20	off	12	(2-4-2)	4	9	2	[+0]Total=55
Week Five*	15 to 20	off	3	5	3	7	3	[+0]Total=36-41

SCHEDULE B

	Day 1	Day 2	Day 3	Day 4	Day 5	Day 6	Day 7	
Week One	18	off	9	(2-4-2)	2	9½	3½	[+0]Total=50 miles
Week Two	18	2	10	(1-5TT-1)	3	10	3½	[+1½]Total=55
Week Three	20	2	11	(2-5-2)	3	11	4	[+0]Total=60
Week Four	20	2	12	(2-5-2)	3	12	3	[+0]Total=61
Week Five*	15 to 20	off	4	6	3	8	3	[+0]Total=37-42

SCHEDULE C: VERY HEAVY, NOT FOR FIRST-TIME MARATHONERS

	Day 1	Day 2	Day 3	Day 4	Day 5	Day 6	Day 7	
Week One	20	3½	12	(2-5-2)	3	13	3	[+0]Total=63½ mi
Week Two	20	3¾	13¼	(2½-5TT-2)	3½	14½	3½	[+0]Total=68
Week Three	20	4	15	(2½-5-2½)	4	15½	3½	[+0]Total=72
Week Four	20	4	15	(2½-5-2½)	5	16	5	[+0]Total=75
Week Five*	15 to 20	off	5	7	4	8	3	[+0]Total=42-47

You can add days together and split them any way you want. In Schedule C: Week 4, the second day is 4 miles and the fifth and seventh days are both 5 miles for a total of 14 miles. What you could do is use 2 miles on the second day, leaving 12. Then use 7 of those on the fifth day (3 in the morning, 4 in the evening split). On the seventh day you may do 3 miles in the morning and only 2 in the evening. This would leave you rested for the next day's run.

You can even use this system to create "off days." Week Two of Schedule B has 2 miles for the second day, 3 for the fifth and 3¼ for the seventh, plus an extra 1½ for a total of 9¾. You could take day two off, split 2 and 3 miles on day five and a 3 mile/2 mile split on day seven; and if you like, remove a half mile from one of your other runs.

Were you surprised to find that this Step had five weeks instead of four and that the fifth week was so very short? Consider it a gift.

Since you've been carefully monitoring your diet, this final surge in training has probably trimmed your body weight down to or near your target. If you still have a pound or so to lose or want to get slightly below-weight to compensate for what you may gain during carbohydrate loading, this is *absolutely your last chance*.

Except for the first day, Week Five is relatively light compared to what you have become used to so you will have to guard carefully against gaining weight. Because your work load has been decreased somewhat your system can now get along with less energy input. The purpose of the light week is to enable you to hold a level of fitness while resting the body in preparation for the big event.

To hold your weight and/or lose a little, all you really have to do is watch the fat, cut back on all portions slightly (except for green salads) and rigorously avoid junk. All your carbohydrates should be in the form of natural foods: wheat germ (if you have no allergies to it), whole wheat bread, natural unsugared yogurt and so on. Stay away from anything with added sugar—no honey and no dried fruit, which has too high a concentration of sugars. Don't allow yourself to get weak, but a slightly hungry feeling is okay.

If you start to get too hungry, have a little yogurt and maybe a bit of bread. Nuts are a great food, but this week consider them too high in oil.

This cutting-back period should last between Sunday and Friday of the fifth week. By then if you aren't weighing what you want to, don't worry, your training will carry you through.

Eat normally Saturday, just don't stuff yourself. You have only a short jog that day, so you can spend as much time as you wish stretching, goofing off and talking running with your friends.

Sunday the week before the marathon is your last long training run. If you are on Schedule A it should be from 8 to 10 miles; Schedule B, 10 to 12 miles; Schedule C, 10 to 15 miles.

Do all your regular stretching and limbering on Sunday and have a good breakfast: fruit, protein, ample carbohydrate. Eat as much as you want, just don't leave the table feeling full.

Sometime Sunday you will do your long run, which is the first step in your carbohydrate depletion schedule. Your diet following the Sunday run through Tuesday night must be strictly regulated.

Monday take a jog of from 5 to 7 miles, depending on your energy level. Tuesday try for 5 miles. If you are on the strict depletion diet, by Tuesday's run you may feel crummy, but you will probably be able to go the 5.

Wednesday. Most people who stick it out this far will feel weak, washed out and devoid of energy. Some may have slight headaches. But take heart. As soon as you finish Wednesday's jog you will be able to *STUFF YOURSELF*. For full details on this glorious prospect, see Chapter V on techniques for Carbohydrate Loading.

Wednesday morning, attempt a 5-mile jog. After you get calmed down, washed off and ready, you can begin Carbohydrate Loading.

This schedule presumes that you started with a Sunday morning long run for depletion. If your Sunday run was in the evening, your Wednesday jog and Carbohydrate Packing is also to be in the evening.

Training for *this* marathon is now over. What we are doing now is storing energy for the big moment.

Thursday jog 2 to 4 miles, no more. Friday do not run at all unless you are very nervous, then do a mile or so of jog/walking. Do your stretches and limbering on Friday as you always do.

Here's the final week's schedule.

Schedule	Sunday	Monday	Tuesday	Wednesday	Thursday	Friday
A	8 to 10	5	5 (?)	5 (?)	2 to 3	-0-
B	10 to 12	5 to 7	5 (?)	5 (?)	2 to 3	-0-
C	10 to 15	5 to 7	5 (?)	5 (?)	3 to 4	-0-

Friday evening before the marathon have a light meal, low in animal protein, low in fat. I usually have a small plate of spaghetti with tomato and mushroom sauce, a small salad, a couple of pieces of garlic toast and a glass of wine.

What about Friday night? Sleep has been very important during your training, especially over the last few high-intensity months. Many people who normally get along all right on 6 or 7 hours of sleep a night suddenly feel the need for 8, 9 or more hours when their miles go up. During the last week before a marathon try to get all the sleep you feel you need. Rest and sleep are not the same. I mean cut some real ZZZZzzzz during the week because you might not get them Friday night.

The Perfect Marathon — Part I

An unfortunate error many first-time marathoners make is trying, Trying, TRYING to get a lot of sleep the night before the race. Usually they jump in bed early, toss and turn until 3 or 4 in the morning and finally drop into a fitful doze only to be awakened by the alarm at 6 a.m.

The best plan I've found is to get adequate sleep during the week. The night before the marathon I get into bed with a book, TV or whatever, and no plans at all for *trying* to fall asleep. If sleep comes, great. It it doesn't come, that's the breaks. Since it isn't being forced, it always seems to come.

The hour you get up on Saturday morning is far more important than the hours you slept the night before.

If the race is to be at 9 a.m., I get up no later than 6 a.m., three hours before race time. As soon as I awake I eat a small banana, drink a small can of unsweetened grapefruit juice and a cup of black coffee from my thermos. Things should be simple. At home or at a motel, I get things ready in advance . . . and that means coffee in a thermos.

I do some light stretching, go to the bathroom, do some more stretching, go to the bathroom, take a warm bath, go to the bathroom and do some more stretching. By then it's probably 6:45. I suit up and go outside to walk and jog a bit...only a few yards at a time. Just enough to get my system moving and keep from getting nervous. I stick close to the bathroom and use it frequently.

I have another cup of black coffee around 7:30 and a final cup a little after eight...one hour before the race—very important.

I spend the last few minutes in the bathroom, then leave for the race site, arriving 30 to 40 minutes before the start. No earlier. If you arrive sooner you'll find yourself waiting behind 150 people for your turn at the portable outhouse.

I always pre-register for the race, sometimes weeks or months in advance. If that isn't possible I will certainly register the night before. *Never wait to register the morning of the race.*

As soon as I get to the site I pick up my number and pin it on, grease the insides of my thighs, under my arms and my paps with Vaseline and go for a jog. That's right. Thirty minutes before a marathon, I'm out jogging.

"JOGGING JUST BEFORE A MARATHON? YOU MUST BE NUTS!"

You know, just about everybody says that. Hah, let them eat dust. This is no ordinary running book. We've got some real honest-to-goodness training secrets here.

When you first start running at an aerobic pace there's an initial build-up of lactic acid. If you continue at an aerobic pace the level of lactic acid drops almost to the state it was before you began. The idea of the pre-race run is to get the system really warmed up: capillaries dilated, lactic acid level up and coming down, all this using less energy than someone standing around worrying about the event.

When the gun goes off you are going to run the first mile effortlessly while most of the other runners, no matter how much they stretched, are going to do that mile on rusty stalks.

So jog very slowly for about 15 minutes, out and back. About halfway through, veer into the woods, if necessary, to take a final leak (or tinkle, depending on your gender or vocabulary). I *always* find it necessary to veer off.

It should now be about 10 minutes or so until race time, but I have yet to see a race start on time. Wait until practically the last moment before you get into the mob, and when you do it is important to place yourself.

It is usually suggested that if you expect to finish in the middle, you should start in the middle, and so on. I haven't found this to be good advice. If you start in the middle it's going to be several minutes before you can break out of the crowd and establish your stride and pace. Besides, there will be a bunch of hotshots trying to climb over your back to get past you no matter where you are; hotshots who will probably be walking by the 10 or 15-mile mark. Get up near the front, but don't get in the way of the champs. The front 25% of the pack is fine.

So here you are, all trained to a fine edge. Your rub points are all greased, your running outfit is festive, and your shoes are fashionably scuffed. Your number is pinned securely to your singlet and you are springing from toe to toe listening for the gun. BUT WAIT.

How are you going to run this race of your life? You've trained the best you can and that's behind you. Better forget it, nothing you can do now to make up for what you may have missed then. Look ahead.

You will succeed or suffer on the basis of tactics. *The Perfect Marathon* can be yours. Don't let it slip from your grasp.

Step 12 Notes

- Have you been training consistently for months, perhaps a year or more? Is your resting pulse slow and steady? Are you as lean or leaner than you have ever been in your life? Are you packed full of energy and excitement? Are you focused strongly on a marathon about six weeks from now? YES! Then this is the step for you!

- Step 12 is not for training. Training has been completed. Now is the time for fine tuning, planning and direct race preparation. Step 12 includes 4 weeks of high-level running to maintain fitness and speed, one all-important week of rest and recuperation, and finally the tapering-off race week which includes an optional carbohydrate depletion and loading schedule.

- During this 6-week period it is *extremely important* to get ample sleep, at least 8 hours, and towards the end some runners require 10 to 12 hours per night.

The Perfect Marathon — Part I

- You are already a highly trained distance runner and almost a marathoner. You understand training, you have learned to "read your body," and you have a good grasp of your potential .. don't blow it. Now is not the time to experiment! Don't change running shoes for some new wonder that's just hit the market. Don't try some secret training trick or some "magic" innovation. Save the experiments for later. For now stick with the old familiar; follow the race week schedule and plan your actual race carefully; you will be amazed and thrilled with the results.

Training Log: 7-Day/5-Week Schedule

WEEK 1

	DAY 1	DAY 2	DAY 3	DAY 4	DAY 5	DAY 6	DAY 7	7 DAY TOTAL
Daily Mileage								
Comments								
	AM / PM	AM / PM	AM / PM	AM / PM	AM / PM	AM / PM	AM / PM	WEIGHT
Pulse								

WEEK 2

	DAY 1	DAY 2	DAY 3	DAY 4	DAY 5	DAY 6	DAY 7	7 DAY TOTAL
Daily Mileage								
Comments								
	AM / PM	AM / PM	AM / PM	AM / PM	AM / PM	AM / PM	AM / PM	WEIGHT
Pulse								

Training Log: 7-Day/5-Week Schedule

WEEK 3

	DAY 1	DAY 2	DAY 3	DAY 4	DAY 5	DAY 6	DAY 7	7 DAY TOTAL
Daily Mileage								
Comments								
	AM | PM	AM | PM	AM | PM	AM | PM	AM | PM	AM | PM	AM | PM	WEIGHT
Pulse								

WEEK 4

	DAY 1	DAY 2	DAY 3	DAY 4	DAY 5	DAY 6	DAY 7	7 DAY TOTAL
Daily Mileage								
Comments								
	AM | PM	AM | PM	AM | PM	AM | PM	AM | PM	AM | PM	AM | PM	WEIGHT
Pulse								

Training Log: 7-Day/5-Week Schedule

WEEK 5

	DAY 1		DAY 2		DAY 3		DAY 4		DAY 5		DAY 6		DAY 7		7 DAY TOTAL
Daily Mileage	AM	PM	AM	PM	AM	PM	AM	PM	AM	PM	AM	PM	AM	PM	
Comments															
Pulse															WEIGHT

The Race and the Rest

RUNNING the RACE:

TACTICS

Chapter I

The Perfect Marathon is within your grasp. You've trained and prepared. Now it's time to plan the battle tactics.

Remember the *Time Trial* during the second week of Step Twelve? Your time for that 5 miles is one of the most important tools you have in your quest for success.

Most people enter their first marathon without the slightest idea of what pace they should follow. They either go out too fast at the start and ruin their chances of finishing, or they go out too slowly, prolonging the agony, and increasing the likelihood that they will be forced to walk some of the distance. You will be able to avoid both these problems.

There is a direct relationship between your ability to run 5 miles at a given pace and your ability to run 26.2 miles at a given pace. If certain variables are taken into account, your 5 mile Time Trial results and the Marathon Predictor Chart can be used to obtain a most efficient pace for your 26.2 miles.

First, complete the following series of questions. For every "Yes" answer, enter a zero. For every "No," enter 1.

Have you ever finished a marathon? . . . . _____
(If this is your first marathon, or if you have entered one before but didn't finish, count this as "no" and mark one.)

Have you run a 20-Miler this month? . . . . _____

The Perfect Marathon — Part II

Have you run two or more 20-Milers during the past month? _____
(If you only ran one, mark 1.)

Have you ever finished a marathon? . . . . ._____
(If this is your first marathon or if you have entered one before but didn't finish, count this as no and mark 1.)

Have you run a 20-Miler this month? . . . . ._____

Have you run two or more 20-milers during the past month? ._____
(If you only ran one, mark 1.)

During the last 5 weeks of training did you run three or more 20-Milers? . . . . ._____
(If you only ran two, mark 1.)

Is the marathon being held on a flat course? . . . . ._____
(If there are any hills, mark 1.)

Is this marathon being held in cool weather? . . . . ._____
(If the temperature is expected to get over 75°, mark 1.)

Were you on Schedule B or C? . . . . ._____
(If you were on A, mark 1.)

Were you on Schedule C? . . . . ._____
(If you were on A or B, mark 1.)

Note: If you were on Schedule A, you count 1 for both of the last two questions.

If you were overweight at the start, do you believe you've reduced enough? . . . . ._____
(Be honest now, can you grab a blob of fat?)

Add up all your ones and multiply by five. This is your chart total. If you counted 1 mark for the second question (no 20-Milers at all), add another 5 points to get the final total.

Turn to the Marathon Predictor chart in the back of the book and find your time for the 5-Mile TT in the left-hand column. These figures are rounded off, so if you can't find your exact time use the next slower on the list. Now move down the column as many positions as the questionnaire total.

If, for example, your time was 40:00 for five miles and you had a total of 20 points on the questionnaire, you'd go down 20 lines to 45:00. Simple, huh?

Found your correct spot? OK. Now trace across to the third column—your predicted marathon time. If you have really trained, and if you pace yourself correctly, you have a very good chance to finish in the predicted time or even a bit sooner.

Now that you have a marathon finish time, what do you do with it? Boy, I'm glad you asked!

For the purposes of illustration only, let's assume your 5-mile time was 34:00 and you had ten points, giving you a corrected time of 36:30. If you move across to the marathon time you will find this will give you a 3:30 finish. By going over one more column you find the per-mile average for a 3:30 marathon is approximately 8 minutes (8:015). If you run every one of the 26.2 miles at an 8 minute pace you will finish comfortably under three and a half hours.

114

Before race time, use this system to find your own personal corrected marathon prediction, noting both the finish time and the per-mile time. Now move over one more column. This takes you into the splits. On a roll of *wide* adhesive tape, use an indelible pen or marker to write down your predicted finish, per-mile pace and splits for 5, 10, 15, 20 and 25 miles. Make the numbers clear and large enough to read comfortably. When you need them most your brain won't be computing too well.

Put the tape on your wrist sweat band so it can be easily checked. In addition to carrying the splits on tape you will also need a wrist stopwatch or chronometer. I prefer one with a digital readout but a standard face with hands will also serve. Whichever type you use, make sure it will accumulate at least 60 minutes. Thirty minute totals can get confusing.

Why all this talk about splits? An examination of thousands of marathon times points out that while it is not often achieved, the even pace has its rewards, and there are penalties for greatly exceeding pace.

A good illustration of pacing is Ron Tabb's fine performance at the 6th Annual Houston Marathon. Competing in subfreezing weather, Ron won the race in 2:17:11.

Starting the race with a modest burst, Ron finished the first 5 miles with an average pace that exceeded his total race pace by 8 seconds. Then he settled in and his average pace between the 5 and 10 mile marks was within 2 seconds of race pace. Between 10 and 15 miles he was averaging within 1 second of race pace. Fantastic! Between 15 and 20 miles he picked up 7 seconds on his average and paid for the extravagance by dropping back 15 seconds on his average from 20 to 25 miles - won.7, paid for it with 15 seconds per mile for 5 miles. A loss of 1:15. Between 25 miles and the finish, Ron was back on target with an *average within 1 second of race pace*.

Another fine runner in that same race had a 25 mile to finish pace that was a *minute and a half slower* than race pace - pace is always a mile average. After a fast start and a very even first 10 miles, his times became progressively slower. His average for the 5 to 10 miles was actually *faster* than the winner's, but his average for 25 miles to the finish was almost 2 minutes slower than the winner's time.

It's much too easy to second-guess, but after examining the computer printouts, it seems that this runner might have been able to *improve his overall time* by running 5 or 6 seconds per mile slower at the beginning of the race. This would have helped even out his pace and might have prevented the "crash" that came in the final 6.2 miles. If this strategy had worked, this runner would have finished at least one place closer to first.

115

The Perfect Marathon — Part II

The first two finishers did their final 1.2 miles very close to race-pace. Places 3 through 6 did their final 1.2 miles from 29 seconds to a minute and a half slower than race pace. It appears that the speed you use early has to be paid back at least double toward the end.

When you run your first marathon, it is important that you don't burn yourself out early. Follow the pace you have calculated, but you don't have to be fanatical…this is ample cushion built in.

Armed with your months of training, a realistic predicted time and your written splits, you will prevail. Your times won't be exactly even, but they will be close. Your final mile will probably be even faster than some of those in the middle and chances are you may finish even sooner than you planned.

Enough of splits and pace, let's get to race day.

You finally fell asleep around 10 and woke up just before the alarm at 6 a.m. You feel wonderful, refreshed but a little nervous…you head for the bathroom. Now you're a little less nervous.

It takes you 20 minutes to slowly eat your banana and drink your juice, partially because you've made four more trips to the bathroom.

You're now lounging in a warm bath having already finished your morning stretches.

You dress in your running gear and go out to take a walk, 5 minutes later you're back in the bathroom. Out you go for another walk. About quarter to eight you're back in the bathroom for the hundredth time…better now than on the course.

At eight o'clock you sip a cup of coffee while knocking on the adjoining hotel room door to make sure your buddies are ready. They are. In fact, they wanted to get to the race site 2 hours early, but not you. You know better. Off you head for one last visit to the pit.

It's 8:30. You are greased up, your number is trimmed and fastened to your singlet. Your splits are taped to your wristband, and you and your friends are slowly jogging away from the race site. You meet a few other people with numbers who are jogging, but most folks are standing around looking nervous, or standing in line at the outhouses looking nervous.

A few minutes later you veer off from the group toward a clump of trees to take a last leak. Your friends, if they have any sense, are also heading for the woods.

Together again, you jog slowly back to the start of the race. The crowds are gathering and some competitors are lining up behind the start. But not you, there's still 10 minutes to go.

Only minutes to the gun and you scramble to get out of your sweats and hand them to a friend. You press into the milling throng near the front, but behind the really fast runners.

The gun goes off. The crowd explodes and you click your watch. Behind you the runners are bunched together; some still haven't crossed the starting line; some are even walking. You're in full stride. Ahead the champs are pulling away and a few runners are passing you, but mostly they are all around and you're holding your own.

Adrenaline is burning through your body and you're so excited your head is ready to burst. You're going much too fast and you try to hold back.

It seems as if you just started but, there's the one-mile mark. You glance at your watch. You're 30 seconds ahead of schedule. Nothing to worry about. Your body is settling in fine and you reign in your pace slightly.

You're still practically out of your skull with the excitement of the event—hardly aware of what's going on around you—as you reach the 3-mile mark and an unofficial water stop.

You grab a cup of water, walk a couple of paces drinking and begin to run again. Were you the only one to stop and drink? Who cares!

You are finally in control as you approach the 5-mile mark, and again you glance at your watch. You're now 45 seconds ahead of schedule. Very good, your pace is settling down. Now you're free to look about and enjoy the race. The roadway is lined with hundreds of people; some looking on in dumbstruck awe, others waving with excitement. An elderly woman leans out from her car and calls sweetly, "What are all you nice young people doing? Is this some kind of protest?" You wave at her and smile.

People are passing you on both sides. You'll notice that most of them are a little overweight, their shirts have cute sayings on them ("I may be slow but I'm way ahead of you") and their shoes are suspiciously new looking. Don't worry, let them pass. You'll be seeing them again before long.

Although you occasionally retreat inside your own head and at other times are laughing and joking with other runners or the crowd, you still remember to check your watch every mile. You're picking up about 5 seconds each checkpoint. Wonderful. Couldn't be better.

You pass the 10-mile mark still riding the peak and feel a rush of joy...you're 1:10 ahead of schedule. At the eleven mile mark you notice you've picked up an additional 15 seconds. Too fast. You cut back ever so slightly. At 12 miles you are smack on pace, but still a minute and 25 seconds ahead of schedule.

You're slowly slipping into a hypnotic trance but pull out of it as you pass the 13-mile mark - you picked up less than a couple of seconds this time. As you approach the 14-mile mark you call "It's more than half over!" There are several groans and one runner becomes a walker.

You're feeling great. Fourteen miles. Nothing to it. Why, you run further than that every Sunday.

At fifteen miles you are right on pace again but now a minute and 35 seconds ahead of schedule. Your pace is so regular you are being lulled deeper into a trance-like state. You snap out of it as you approach the 16-mile mark...no, it's the 17-mile mark. You have been completely out of touch for two miles. You glance at your watch. You've lost 45 seconds.

"I must have been practically crawling," you think to yourself. But you've still got a 50-second lead on your predicted time. You up your pace slightly and pass the 18-mile mark one minute ahead of schedule.

117

The Perfect Marathon — Part II

You're feeling light and running without effort. You pass a water stop. This is the first one you've ignored. At 19 miles you are right on pace and at 20 miles you pick up another 5 seconds. You are now 1:05 ahead of schedule.

People are walking and limping, moaning and groaning all around you. You attempt to joke with those running near you but no one feels like laughing. So you laugh at your own joke.

At 21 you pick up a couple of seconds and at 22 you again pick up 5. You are now a minute and a quarter ahead of your own schedule and feeling fantastic.

Not many runners around now, but lots of walkers spread out along the road. It suddenly dawns on you that there wasn't a wall. What *is* the wall?

You are passing the 24-mile mark and the crowds are getting thicker and screaming hysterically. You've never run more than 20 miles in your life and here you are passing the 24-mile mark and feeling invincible.

Up ahead you can see the flags waving. People reach out to touch you. "You're almost there," they cry out, "don't give up." You wouldn't even dream of giving up.

THE FINISH IS A NEW BEGINNING

Chapter II
Recover - Advance - Experiment

Turn on the power and burn your way through. The officials are there to pull the dawdlers out of the way and let you come tearing in and out the other side. DON'T STOP.

Let your momentum hurtle you along after you shut off. Grandstand! You worked for it and you deserve it.

RECOVERY. Keep jogging a little if you are able, but at least keep walking or your legs are going to draw up.

Let your friends help you. You may have to lower your head for a few seconds to keep from keeling over, but don't stop moving and don't lie down.

Once your breathing is normal and you're pretty sure you are not going to cramp, you can finally get off your feet. If it feels good and somebody wants to do it, a leg massage would help at this point.

As soon as you are able, get up and start walking again. You might even *try* some very easy stretches…anything to keep from cramping.

By now someone should have brought you something to drink - water, Coke or beer - at least a quart. No need for me to tell you to drink…your body will crave liquid right after the race. A little later you may develop a craving for . . . but you won't have the strength.

After a race I drink everything cold—in summer very cold; and when I get to the beer, it isn't the light stuff. I like my beer as heavy and dark as I can get it. What you drink is up to you.

If you have run a good evenly-paced race, and have finished well within your capabilities, your legs should be in pretty good shape by that evening…but you *will* be aware of them.

As you and your friends are lounging around the hotel that afternoon, you may notice an interesting phenomenon—your calves walking of their own accord—even though you aren't moving. I won't explain further, but when it happens *you'll know it*.

In the afternoon you will *feel* wonderful, but be sure to have someone take plenty of pictures so you can relive the occasion and see what you *actually* looked like.

The Perfect Marathon — Part II

In the pictures you will see a happy person who has finished running 26.2 miles, plus a mile and a half. You will see an exhausted, wacked out and drained body, and a face glowing with a smile of ecstacy. It was worth it; you are already beginning to plan for the next one.

Try to do a good deal of walking on Saturday—short, little walks, even up and down stairs if possible—and try to get in some stretching. Sunday you should try to get in even more walking and a little stretching, but no straining.

Monday tells the tale. I've run races on a Saturday and afterwards was so stiff I had to walk up stairs backwards for three days. But there have been other times . . .

After my first marathon I suffered from cramping for about a half-hour, then the legs began to clear up. By the time we got to the hotel I was able to walk slowly up a flight of stairs and by the evening I was able to walk the stairs comfortably. Sunday I was able to bound up and down, skipping several stairs at a time. My more experienced friends were still limping and not liking me a bit.

Monday I went out for a short jog. At three miles when I was about to quit, I said to myself, "Wait a minute, Schreiber! You're a marathoner. You can do anything!" I went on to jog 15 miles. I did 40 that week, 50 the next, then 60 and 65. My long runs were the 15 already mentioned, an 18 and two 20s. Then I did a 10-miler with a short week and ran my second marathon.

This second race became my first Perfect Marathon. I finished 20 minutes faster than the first time with much less effort. I continued training as before, but just a little harder - perhaps a little too hard.

The third marathon was in below-freezing weather, which felt wonderful, and again it was a Perfect Marathon. Again, the finish was about 20 minutes faster than the previous one, and again, I seemed to have expended less energy.

Unfortunately I had overtrained *just prior* to the third race and went into it with a sore hamstring in one leg. After that race I was out of commission for a couple of weeks. Not really injured, just very sore and mentally and physically wiped out...even so, I still felt it had been worth it.

I had hoped to run a couple of more marathons, but I just couldn't get it together until the next season. Even so, three marathons in three months wasn't bad for a beginner.

I'm not suggesting you try the same trick, but it does seem to have some training validity and logic to it.

First you lay down a long-term base on which to build your first marathon - steps 0 through 12. That base takes one year or longer to construct.

Considering your abilities in the shorter distances (5-mile Time Trial), the realities of your training and the look of the course, you make an objective estimate of your marathon time.

Pacing yourself correctly, you complete your first Perfect Marathon. You have prepared so well that you have finished uninjured with both spirits and expectations high. Not only have you run a marathon, but you have run the longest mileage in your career and it was much easier than training.

ADVANCE! There is another marathon 5 weeks away, close enough to keep your enthusiasm at a raging peak.

You take a complete day off to allow your body to begin to recover and for your muscles to replace some of their lost glycogen. Then you go into light training which keeps your muscles well-flushed and well-supplied with nourishment.

Still in fantastic tone, the second week you up your mileage to 50 . . . nothing for an athlete who has done over 26 miles in a single run. The following week you do 60, then 65 and down to a 40-45 mile week to give the body a rest.

Now you go into the depletion/packing stage and it's marathon time again. But this time you have *double the number of 60+ mile weeks under your shoes, double the number of 18-mile runs, double the number of 20s, plus a 28-mile day* (counting the jog before your first marathon).

Not only are you going into the second marathon better prepared in total mileage, long runs and *experience*, but you've also had two low mileage rest weeks - one after the first race and one just before the second.

Again I must say that I am not advising you to run successive marathons within a short period of time; it can really put a strain on your system if you're not extremely careful. For some this is a route to rapid advancement, for others...disaster.

If you plan to wait six months to a year before your next race, you should probably cut back to a maintenance level of 30 to 40 miles per week and a long run that varies between 8 and 15 miles. Give yourself enough time to work back up to a month of 60 or more miles per week and at least two 18-milers and two 20-milers.

You should allow enough lead time so you don't have to increase more than 10% per week - less is even better.

As you become more experienced and as your training base deepens you will probably go the route of ever-increasing mileage. I know many runners who, starting at 50 miles per week, creep up to 80, 90, 100 and more per week, finally reaching 500 miles and more per month.

This ever-increasing mileage may eventually reach the point of diminishing returns with chronic exhaustion and chronic glycogen depletion outweighing the positive effects of the training. This point of diminishing returns may not be reached by everyone who trains long distances, but it is reached by some, and some of the best.

You'll recall the acquaintance of mine who regularly trained 150 miles per week when he was feeling good and only 120 when he was feeling poorly. Well, he had never realized that he was chronically tired until outside forces kept him from completing a week's training just before a race. After the race he commented that he had felt years younger, and that it was the first race he could remember entering where he felt refreshed before the start.

It may seem strange, but there are runners who can accomplish 40, 50, 60, perhaps 70 mile-weeks that other runners have to train 120 - 150 per week to accomplish. Why? Quite simply, we are all different - but it has been suggested that the only good reason for really long training weeks is to keep the weight down. So, if you have no trouble keeping your body weight pared and if you easily achieve that lean and hungry look on 70 miles per week or less, *perhaps* you don't need to run 20 to 25 miles every day.

TRAINING EXPERIMENT. If you haven't received the benefits you want from long training weeks, or if you've decided you don't want to take the long route in the first place, you may be interested in an *experimental* regime.

Before you start on either phase of this experimental system you should have experience with at least one marathon, preferably several, over two or more seasons. You *must* also be completely adapted to long daily runs of 15 to 20 miles. Even fulfilling these criteria, you should still work into this experimental program over the period of a month or longer.

The experiment is based on two ideas, one a *factoid* and the other a supposition.

First the supposition. If you have been a long-distance runner for many years without a break, you have received just about all the benefit you are going to get from short runs (except those used instead of days off and for TT). Long runs are what you really need.

Now the *factoid*. Long runs burn up a lot of muscle glycogen, and it takes much longer than overnight to replace it. Therefore, successive long runs over a period of time - as in 500+, 600+ mile months - can cause chronic glycogen depletion and result in a negative training effect.

What this program does is provide for plenty of long runs while still allowing for the replacement of glycogen reserves. There are two possible levels of intensity.

The Perfect Marathon — Part II

LEVEL ONE

	Day 1	Day 2	Day 3	Day 4	Day 5	Day 6	Day 7	Total
Week One*	20	off	15	off	15	off	15	65 miles
Week Two	off	20	off	15	off	15	off	50 miles
	off	Two consecutive days off after every 2 weeks.						
Week Three	15	off	20	off	15	off	15	65 miles
Week Four	off	15	off	20	off	15	off	50 miles
	off	Two consecutive days off after every 2 weeks.						

LEVEL TWO

	Day 1	Day 2	Day 3	Day 4	Day 5	Day 6	Day 7	Total
Week One	20	off	15	off	20	off	15	70 miles
Week Two	off	20	off	15	off	20	off	55 miles
	off	Two consecutive days off after every 2 weeks.						
Week Three	15	off	20	off	15	off	20	70 miles
Week Four	off	15	off	20	off	15	off	50 miles
	off	Two consecutive days off after every 2 weeks.						

*These are not calendar weeks but workout periods of seven days.

NOTE: In both levels one and two there are 2 off days at the end of each second week. One of these double days off can be changed to a short jog of 2 or 3 miles.

In Level One we have 20-mile days followed by three 15-mile days, all of them alternating with off days. This results in alternating seven day periods of 65 and 50 miles per week, not counting the added off day every second week.

In Level Two we have alternating 20-mile days and 15-mile days divided by off days. This give alternating 70-mile and 55-mile seven day periods, not counting the extra off day every other period.

122

Both of these levels incorporate a *double hard/easy pattern*. You might consider 20/15 miles as hard/easy, but I'd call that very hard/hard. The second part of the double whammy is the hard/easy alternating weeks. You can even turn this into a triple whammy by starting with Level One and then switching over to Level Two.

One way to use this system in preparation for a marathon: start with Level One, do a 50-mile week, a 65-miler (2 days off), a 50-miler, a 65-mile week, and then switch to Level Two. Then do a 55 and a 70-mile week (2 days off), 55 miles, 70 miles (2 days off). Finally, do a 40-mile week, the carbohydrate loading week and the marathon.

This results in 8½ weeks of heavy training, a light week and the marathon week. There's a total of seventeen 15-mile runs and twelve 20 milers. There are also two 50-mile weeks, two 55s, two 65s and two 70-milers, all run on an alternating hard/easy basis.

This experiment offers the advantages of lots of rest days, lots of long runs and weekly totals far from the extravagant level some runners are forcing themselves to reach...yet 50 to 70 miles per week is nothing to sneeze at.

By the time you reach this point, not in your reading but in your training, you will be your own expert. I am not encouraging you to try this training method. I am only suggesting that training can be an adventure. If you do attempt something like this or something of your own devising, it will be your own decision and perhaps your own feeling for adventure that leads you on.

Chapter III
Watching Your Breath Mildew

Most trainers advise giving up training if the temperature is above 90^0 or the humidity is above 80%. I think that's great, because it's really miserable to be out on the road with the flesh oozing off your bones. But what if it just happens to be summer and you just happen to live in Texas, Louisiana, Florida or some other swamp? Do you give up training for three or four months?

Suppose your job is transferred from one of the coasts or from the Moderate Midwest to the Muggy South. Are you going to have to pack in your training for a third of the year? NO. Running may not be as easy or as much fun during the hottest, most humid days of the summer, but it can be done.

Jim Lindsey tells me that he actually looks forward to the summer when it's hot enough to melt brass and humid enough to mildew your eyeballs. He says the sauna-like atmosphere benumbs his mind and makes the miles go faster.

I occasionally run with Jim at 5:50 in the afternoon with the sun beating full in our faces. It's hell, and 5 miles is harder for me then than 20 was during the winter. Doesn't bother Jim at all. After one of these runs I flopped down on a lawn chair with a beer, while he lifted weights for half an hour. Was he putting on an act? We'll never know.

For the rest of us crazy summer runners the combination of heat and humidity can be not only a joy killer; but it can also be lurking danger, threatening us with dehydration, heat exhaustion and brain baking.

Except for the times I run with Lindsey, I pick my hours carefully. Early in the morning, before sunup, is usually the coolest...probably 10^0 cooler than any other part of the day. Unfortunately, I

124

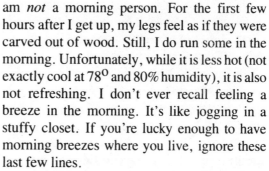

am *not* a morning person. For the first few hours after I get up, my legs feel as if they were carved out of wood. Still, I do run some in the morning. Unfortunately, while it is less hot (not exactly cool at 78° and 80% humidity), it is also not refreshing. I don't ever recall feeling a breeze in the morning. It's like jogging in a stuffy closet. If you're lucky enough to have morning breezes where you live, ignore these last few lines.

My favorite time to train is about 11 o'clock at night. At that hour it is almost as cool (?) as in the morning and there is frequently a breeze, which makes it very nice…comparatively speaking, of course.

This summer I've been running at 7:30 in the evening. It's rough for about an hour, then a breeze comes up about 8:30. I continue jogging after that and it's usually pretty nice.

Last year my summer routine often consisted of 4 miles in the morning and 5 or 6 miles, or more, in the evening. The night run was the most enjoyable for me and I often drifted into a dreaming state. Others have also told me that late in the dark night was when they most often had their "driftings into other worlds." A word of warning, however: I would caution any woman, or male for that matter, against running alone in the dark or alone in any isolated area even in the daylight. There are creeps out there just waiting to trash your body and scar your mind.

If you must put yourself in a potentially dangerous position, maybe you should carry a can of Mace, or a Freon-powered horn which sounds like a Mack truck, and can be found at a boating supply house. They may help, but I have my doubts. Mace sometimes makes attackers mad rather than knocking them down.

However you decide to protect yourself, through companions, force of arms, staying out in the open or fleetness of foot, the earlier or later your schedule and temperament allow you to train, the more comfortable you'll be.

Creeps and muggers aren't the only nighttime dangers. Invisibility can be a real killer. The usual suggestion is to wear light-colored clothing after dark. Better than nothing, I suppose, but not really effective. "Scotchlite" patches stuck on various parts of the body will alert the passing motorist. A roadworker's reflective tunic works even better. But best, in my opinion, is a couple of bike rider's two-way flashlights...one attached to an arm, the other to a leg. Since dogs are often out at night, I would also suggest you carry a two-foot piece of broom handle with reflective tape at each end. This is **not** for hitting, just for keeping them beyond arm's length. Wait a minute. How did we get on the subject of flashlights, sticks and dogs. Didn't this begin as a discussion on the subject of heat?!

Although you can't get completely away from the heat (unless you use the Y's air-conditioned indoor track) you can put something between you and the environment.

I am aesthetically and ecologically partial to cotton. That's what I use for almost all my training clothes, summer and winter. Last summer, however, I finally broke down and splurged on a pair of nylon jogging shorts with a built-in brief. These shorts cost me four times more than my old cotton ones. However, they weigh about a third less than the cotton shorts, allow perspiration to rapidly evaporate...and do they feel sexy. The ads for some of these types of shorts say that wearing them feels almost like running naked. How true, how true! I still train mostly in cotton shorts, but I do wear the light fancy ones in the marathons, and I take them with me when I travel.

I wear a cotton tank top (singlet) both for training and for racing. Another style of shirt rapidly gaining in popularity, especially for hot weather, is a synthetic that's half fabric and half net. Supposedly the net provides more surface area for cooling. Some runners swear by them, others swear at them, feeling they cling too much in hot/damp weather. One manufacturer claims to have a new fabric or knit that won't cling at all. Sounds good, but I think I'll just stick with my soft-and-comfortable cotton tank tops.

If you are training in the summer for the first time and use a lot of table salt, you will probably wind up with sore, burning eyes after a half hour on the course. That will be from salty sweat pouring off your head, some of it dripping off your eyebrows into your eyes and the rest dripping off the end of your nose onto your shirt.

You should probably try to cut back on extra salt. Many runners and health nuts I know have taken the saltshaker completely off the table. I haven't gone that far yet, but I do use far less salt than I used to.

Another way to keep salt out of your eyes is to wear a headband. They cost a buck or less and you can find them at jogging shops, tennis shops and in the sport section of most department and discount stores. Even a few drugstores carry them. While you're at it, you should probably get a pair of wristbands. Not only do they help absorb perspiration, but they give you something to wipe your nose with.

I always carry a big white handkerchief with me to mop the sweat from my face and neck. If the sun is beating down, you can slip the handkerchief under your headband to reflect the heat and sunlight from the back of your head and neck—just like in the French Foreign Legion. If you don't use a headband, you can use a white T-shirt to make a Foreign Legion hat. Here's how to do it. Hold the shirt by the sleeves and drape it over your shoulders. Fit the neck hole around your forehead and tie the sleeves behind your head. It should look something like an Egyptian headdress—if you use a lot of imagination. This device will do a good job of protecting your head, neck, and back of your shoulders. It will do an even better job if you sprinkle some cold water on it once in a while.

Cold water is the real answer and the real lifesaver. I have a bunch of little gadgets called "wash bottles." They're plastic screw-top containers with tubes coming out of their tops. They come in many different sizes and are available from pharmaceutical supply houses at modest price. You can also get them at sporting goods stores with fancy designs printed on at slightly higher price.

If it's brutally hot (as it usually is where I live) and I am going to run at the track, I fill a number of bottles with ice and water and put them in a bucket with ice. I set the bucket on a chair by the side of the track. As I come around, if I feel the need, I grab a bottle and carry it with me for a quarter of a mile, sipping and dribbling water on my head.

Running In Heat And Humidity

It's usually so hot out, even late in the evening, that if I carry a bottle more than a quarter mile the ice melts and the water gets warm. So I always replace the bottle as soon as I pass the chair again. If I do a ten-mile run all the ice is melted well before I'm finished. This summer I think I'll use an iced styrofoam chest to hold the drinks.

If you're running in the streets (sounds like a 1950's movie), at a park, or along a hike and bike trail, you'll have to take your chances on finding water—unless you stash bottles along the way or are lucky enough to have a trainer hand you a drink from time to time.

If you don't stash and don't have a trainer, there's still something you can do to cool the bod between water fountains. Get a plastic bottle with a spritzer—an old perfume bottle will do—and fill it with ice, water and rubbing alcohol. This is **NOT** for drinking. It's for spritzing on the head, arms, and body, but keep it away from your eyes and nose.

When you are running you will feel hot, but when you stop: you will feel HOT! If you've been training for 40 minutes to an hour or more in the heat, as soon as you stop moving, your temperature will shoot up. The perspiration may actually pour off your body and leave puddles on the ground. Get yourself cooled off FAST. I always stop near running water so I can get some on my face, shoulders, arms and wrists. I want to get my temperature down as fast as I can without actually chilling myself.

While I'm doing all this I also rinse my mouth out several times with cool water and then take a drink. I'll walk around a bit; put some more water *on* and *in* my body… then it's cold-beer-time.

Training In The Cold

Chapter IV
Freezing Your Nikes Off

A blinding northern blizzard! A fur trapper, hands and arms crammed inside the carcass of a freshly killed timber wolf. That's cold, right! Although some marathoners I know would probably train in weather like that, I really wouldn't advise it. It's too easy to get lost on the way home.

Most of my experience outdoors in the cold has been snowshoeing in Vermont at 20°F and 30°F below and backpacking on various mountains in freezing and below-zero weather. I remember waking up one frosty morning to find last night's wine frozen in the bottle. Still, all things considered, northern Vermont or the San Bernardino Mountains at 20° below zero are much more comfortable than the Texas Gulf Coast when it's 100°F and 100% humidity.

For marathoners, cool weather is a blessing. The most comfortable marathon I ever ran was held under slightly-below-freezing conditions. I loved every step, suffered not at all, and my weight-loss from perspiration was too little to measure.

I had trained in cold weather before, but this was my first long race in the cold. I had long experience running and racing in heat.

How to keep from freezing? I tried to find answers in books and from friends but came up with *almost* nothing. So I resorted to my experiences with wilderness camping and backpacking during the winter months. "How," I asked myself, "is running a marathon like backpacking?"

A backpacker must be prepared for all extremes. When you hit the trail in the morning it may be far below zero. You've got to keep warm, but also be able to move comfortably and freely. As the sun comes up the temperature may climb rapidly to the 60s and 70s and you must be able to dissipate that heat—but as you go around an outcropping of rock or move into forest cover, the temperature can drop to below freezing almost instantaneously. "Sounds just like a marathon to me," I thought. "The same kinds of solutions will probably work!" And they did.

Believe it or not, the thing to avoid is heavy clothes. You'll need layers. For moderately cold weather, 20° to 25°F and windless, I wear my regular outfit of shorts and tank top. Over that a thin lightweight, long-sleeved, cotton turtleneck. Over the turtleneck a thin nylon zip-front shell and finally, warm-ups consisting of pants and a zip-front jacket. Please remember, this is all very thin stuff. I wear sweat socks on my hands.

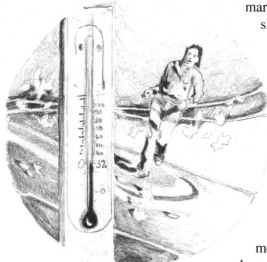

Standing around waiting for the start of my subfreezing marathon, this outfit kept me comfortable, only very slightly chilled.

During the first couple of miles I felt too warm and thought about taking the sweat pants off. Instead, I unzipped the warm-up jacket and nylon shell and put the sweat socks in my pocket. Most of the other runners took off their sweat pants and later regretted it.

After two miles I began to cool down, so I zipped up the shell, leaving the outer jacket to flap. As I rounded a corner the temperature dropped sharply and I put the socks back on my hands. My legs remained perfectly comfortable. While the sweat pants weren't heavy enough to get me overheated, they were just the thing to keep the breeze off my skin.

Throughout the race I kept zipping and unzipping the two outer garments and switching the socks from my hands to my pockets and back again as the temperature changed. Using this method, I was able to stay perfectly comfortable.

The lightweight long-sleeved turtleneck protected me from any cold air that might sneak up the sleeves or down my neck, and it absorbed perspiration. The nylon shell acted as a windbreaker, and the zip-front warm-up jacket acted as the first insulation defense, preventing the nylon from radiating away too much body heat. The sweat socks kept my hands warmer than would either gloves or mittens. Since I have several colorful pairs that don't fit my big feet, socks are a practical as well as efficient solution to cold hands. Because I'm rather long-haired and bearded (those cartoons are really me) my face usually doesn't need any extra protection.

If the weather dropped to 10 or 15 degrees above zero I would probably use the same outfit, but keep it zipped up more and maybe, just maybe, pull the turtleneck up over my nose. Considering my nose, that would be a big pull.

If the weather dropped to between 10 above and 10 below zero, or colder, I'd add a pair of tights under my sweat bottoms and a second long-sleeved cotton shirt, but not a turtleneck. I'd also *consider* using a knit over-the-head ski mask that covered both nose and mouth—but the weather would really have to be *something* before I'd go that far.

If you spray the outside of your clean sweats with several applications of Scotchgard it will help shed moisture

The Perfect Marathon — Part II

and still allow for evaporation. You might also try Scotchgard on new jogging shoes.

Preparing to run in the cold really isn't that big a deal. Just use layers of lightweight, very absorbent material and one layer of windbarrier (my nylon shell). Protect the extremities. Naturally this mean toes, noses, and fingers—but there have also been reports of penile and nipple frostbite, so beware.

When the subfeezing marathon was finished, I went into a huge indoor gathering area with the other runners to drink Coke, eat free yogurt, tell stories and recover. Naturally, as soon as we stopped running we began to sweat. Temperatures went up briefly, then dropped. About 20 minutes later 600 people were shaking and shivering in their damp sweats. Fortunately, some of my friends had the foresight to bring towels and stuff, so I stripped down to my running shorts, toweled off and wrapped up in blankets. I should have have done it much sooner. It was half an hour before I stopped shaking. Sooo...

Just like your mother used to tell you: get out of your damp things as soon as you can, dry off and bundle up...and drink lots of nice hot chicken soup if you can get it. "Now, don't you feel much better?"

Stoking The Fires

Chapter V
Nutrition-Marathoner's Diet-Carbohydrate Loading

Basic Nutrition Nothing is so wrapped up in lies, half-truth, wishful thinking, truth, myth, ritual, ax-grinding, wisdom, nonsense, good sense, no sense, pleasure and disappointment as·the *Cult of Diet*. To get into yet another discussion or argument over the various costs or benefits of one system compared with another would be a fruitless bore.

If one thinks that his/her body is filled with poisons which must be purged through fasting, prunes or mechanical means, that's a personal reality. If one believes that eggs, butter and milk lead to an early grave while non-dairy creamer, artificial breakfast drinks, margarine and corn oil will prolong life, that's also a personal belief that I won't bother challenging.

If you believe that commercial granola is good for you and cupcakes are the exact opposite, that's just fine with me. It's your body, and given the available information and package labeling, you can make your own decisions.

What I want to do is give you a general idea of the type of diet I follow. You can use it, laugh at it, mend it, discard it, or wrap fish.

I'm not what you'd call a moderate or consistent person: my general philosophy is *anything worth doing is worth overdoing*. My diet varies tremendously from week to week and from month to month, but there are a few constants: fresh vegetables, cheese, natural yogurt and fruit.

If you are what you eat, here's what I are. I eat at least a half head of lettuce a day plus tomatoes and cooked greens such as spinach, mustard or turnip tops. Fresh fruit, especially grapefruit, is a must. I often eat peanut butter (no oil or sugar added) mixed with wheat germ, and I am a great consumer of plain natural yogurt, often homemade. When I'm really into it, I make two or three quarts at a time and consume a pint to a quart a day. I make the yogurt from powdered skim milk mixed double or triple rich.

I eat yogurt either straight or mixed with vegetables such as tomatoes and cucumbers, seasoned with salt, pepper and fresh garlic…

The Perfect Marathon — Part II

I *love* V-8 juice and I often mix it with a tablespoon of Super Yeast (with calcium), lemon juice, Worcestershire sauce, salt and pepper. This Super Yeast (Formula 300 by Plus Products) is the best tasting yeast I have ever found...yeast, however, takes some getting used to, so start with a scant teaspoon and work up to a heaping tablespoon.

I buy V-8 by the case. During the few weeks prior to a marathon the V-8/Yeast combination becomes a twice-daily ritual. Also, during the marathon training and anytime colds are going around, I take a basic 1 gram (1000 mg.) of vitamin C. That's basic. For every hour of training I take another gram of C along with plenty of liquids. I also take 1000 I.U.s of vitamin E. I always take the E along with a meal and *never* at the same time as the C. Why? Magic, I guess.

I have this thing against most synthetics. Personally I find the very idea of non-dairy creamer and, to a lesser extent, margarine, kind of nasty. I also stay *almost* completely away from things with added sugar (white, light, tan, brown, dark—any color) and I don't add sugar to things myself—that includes honey.

Regarding sweet things, my only real weakness is ice cream. If I let myself I can eat a half gallon of ice cream at a sitting. I try to reserve such treats for a once-a-week reward for running 10+ miles in the blazing summer heat.

I don't use oils, except for a light brush of olive oil on broiling shrimp, and I make my salads without dressing. What I do use on salads is a modified Caesar.

I mince a garlic clove into fresh cubed tomatoes, season with fresh lemon juice, salt, pepper, MSG, and leave this in a wooden salad bowl at room temperature for a half hour or longer. Crisp broken Romaine (dried and cool) is added and the works tossed with a fresh egg and more seasoning if desired. Grated Parmesan cheese is added as a final garnish.

My diet is very high in cooked and raw vegetables, moderate to high in protein, moderate in carbohydrates, moderate in fat and extremely low in sugar. I have a high intake of B vitamins due to yeast, liver and wheat germ, and good calcium intake from the yeast/calcium supplement, milk and cheese.

I was recently asked to take part in a cardiovascular study comparing marathoners, joggers and sedentary people.

As you read the following, remember that I make no effort to cut back on milk, eggs, beef or pork, but that I *do not add* fat to my diet in the form of oil or spreads. I strictly limit refined carbohydrates, eat natural high fiber food and lots of vegetables.

At the times these tests were made I was not training for a marathon. I was only doing light mileage and I was 10 pounds over my running weight.

Blood pressure was 116/76 and my pulse was 55 (I was a little excited). Then came the blood test—and this was no simple test. The sample was broken down into fasting total cholesterol, fasting total triglycerides and fasting HDL (Alpha) cholesterol. The first two should be as low as possible and the third (HDL) should be high to be good.

My blood test showed FTC at 132 (compared to a study average of 203), FTT at 38 (compared to 106) and HDL at 57, which was better than the ''normal'' of 40 to 50.

Percentage of body fat estimated from skin folds showed 14.552% compared to 16.7% in the study average. Even though this was lower than the average, it reflected my above racing weight. At race time I am about 13% fat, while a really pared-down marathoner is below 10%.

A maximal stress test was included as a part of the study. The treadmill was started level, at a walking pace. Every three minutes the angle and speed were increased. By twelve minutes the surface was at a steep incline and the speed was enough to require a fast run. At fifteen minutes the incline was even steeper and the speed was very fast. My pulse reached an even beating 200+ then leveled out at 208. I terminated the test just under 17 minutes, neither exhausted nor pushed to the extreme. Perhaps if I had been supported by a cheering section I might have stayed on another 2 to 5 minutes . . . perhaps not.

The purpose of including all this information is to back up my belief that it isn't so important to take some specific item from the diet (such as eggs) or add something to the diet such as corn oil. What seems important, to me at least, is to develop a lifestyle that is healthy and wholesome. Such a lifestyle includes activities that progressively strengthen the cardiovascular and muscular systems, a diet that avoids fake stuff and highly refined stuff, and which emphasizes foods that are basic.

In my case eggs certainly didn't elevate cholesterol or triglycerides—but then I eat eggs seasonally. My diet includes a variety of obviously good foods (who's going to argue against lettuce and tomatoes) and I stay away from synthetics and sugar. Let's face it, you can say you like the taste of sugar and fake whipping cream, but deep down inside you are absolutely certain the stuff is rotten for you—you don't need me to convince you.

By the time I have filled up on all the stuff that's good for me, there really isn't much room left for junk. I'll admit I fall off the wagon on ice cream; but my self-serving rationale is I only fall off on occasion and then only when I've paid my dues with an extremely long and difficult workout.

As for the dark beer that I love—fortunately a study claims that three ways have been discovered to elevate HDL in the blood (considered by some to be protection against heart attacks): aerobic exercise (jogging at least 30 minutes and at least 3 times per week); eating fish; and consumption of moderate amounts of non-distilled alcohol (one or two glasses of beer a day or a moderate amount of wine). How fortunate for me.

The added Vitamins C and E I take *may* do me some good (some literature says it will) and I don't see any evidence it hurts. I am well supplied with the B Complex, unlike most Americans. High fiber seems to be the thing these days and I'm okay on that score. Fortunately, I have also been supplied with very good parentage. Thanks Mom and Dad!

133

The Perfect Marathon — Part II

MARATHONER'S ONE WEEK DIET (For experienced runners only.)

Some years ago Dr. Ernst van Aaken developed a powerful one-week diet for experienced marathoners who needed to take weight off quickly. What follows is my version of a one-week pre-competition diet. It is not a casual regimen and should not be used as a general weight control system. It is designed to be used by highly conditioned persons in excellent health who wish to get their weight down prior to an important competition. I use this diet about one month to six weeks before a marathon.

The diet is basically moderate protein, high fiber, moderate carbohydrate with an emphasis on fruit, vegetables and juices with some supplements thrown in. As long as you retain the *idea*, the diet can be changed somewhat to suit your own tastes in food. If you can't tolerate wheat or milk, you will have to make some changes—some people who have trouble with milk have no trouble at all with yogurt.

DAY ONE Six hard-boiled eggs eaten at intervals throughout the day. One quart of juice (apple, orange, grapefruit or V-8) consumed throughout the day. Juice may be cut with water to make it less sweet and to make it last longer. Whole fresh fruit (apples, oranges, grapefruit) may be substituted for some of the juice. Drink plenty of water.

DAY TWO One quart of nonfat unflavored natural yogurt (*or* one quart skim milk with 1½ cups of dry nonfat milk added) eaten throughout the day. 1½ pounds of fresh apples and a pint of juice. Drink plenty of water.

DAY THREE 8 oz. of boiled chicken breast (*or* turkey, veal) eaten in pieces throughout the day. One quart of juice (*or* pint of juice and two medium grapefruit). Two slices of whole wheat bread. Drink plenty of water.

DAY FOUR 8 oz. of chicken liver/calves' liver (*or* six hard-boiled eggs) eaten throughout the day. One quart of juice. Drink plenty of water.

DAY FIVE 8 oz. nonfat cottage cheese eaten throughout the day. 8 oz. of whole wheat bread eaten throughout the day. Drink plenty of water.

DAY SIX 8 oz. of chicken (turkey or veal) eaten throughout the day. Three pounds of apples eaten throughout the day. Drink plenty of water.

DAY SEVEN One quart of natural unflavored yogurt (*or* half yogurt, half whole milk). One quart of juice. Drink plenty of water.

All the food on the daily list, including the juices, should be taken throughout the entire day—from morning until just before bed.

In addition to the foods already listed you should also have daily: a couple of tablespoons of crude bran mixed with a little yogurt, skim milk or juice; a tablespoon or two or Super Yeast (with calcium) mixed with juice: at least a ¼ head of lettuce and chopped celery dressed, if you like, with lemon juice, salt and pepper. I would also continue taking Vitamins C and E, and you might consider taking a multiple vitamin for the week of the diet (I don't).

In order to reduce sweetness and make the liquid last longer, I generally cut fruit juice with water. I drink V-8 cut with lemon juice. Be sure to drink plenty of water and continue to train. Cut back if you get weak.

If you have any doubts about this diet, check with your doctor. Under no circumstances stay on it for longer than 7 days.

Carbohydrate Loading Muscles run on glycogen. The purpose of *Carbohydrate Loading* is to cram at least twice as much glycogen into the muscles as they usually hold.

When runners speak of The Wall, they are generally speaking of a *mythical* point in a race, usually between 16 and 20 miles, when glycogen *will* be used up and the body must switch over to fat metabolism. The usual story is that when the glycogen is used up, there is a sudden feeling of depression and weakness, as if 50-pound bags of sand had replaced the feet. Gradually, as the body begins to utilize fat, some of this depressed feeling lifts.

While it is certainly true that muscle glycogen is used up, I really believe that the major causes of The Wall are: inadequate training (for the speed or distance); poor pacing—particularly early in the race; unrealistic estimation of finish time; and lack of, or incomplete, Carbohydrate Loading.

One must also consider the psychological aspects. If you have been taught to fear The Wall, then beware.

Because there isn't a wall and we have everything going for us, the discussion is moot—but I believe in hedging bets: running as many long runs as possible; getting body weight way down; avoiding injury; estimating a realistic finish time; even pacing. I certainly would also take advantage of Carbohydrate Loading.

Here, basically, is what research seems to show. On a high protein diet (which used to be prescribed for athletes) a given amount of glycogen is stored in the muscles. *On a high carbohydrate diet, the amount of stored glycogen is doubled.* However, if one first starves the body of carbohydrates, then packs it in, *the stored glycogen doubles again.* Fantastic! Not only that, but after a marathon the muscles will still contain twice the glycogen they would have if fed on a highcarbohydrate diet (minus depletion). This could result in faster recovery.

But there is a problem. Muscles won't stay packed with glycogen. Once you get them saturated they turn around and begin to unload. That's *one* of the reasons you may have to urinate so much just before a race: as the body dumps glycogen, water is released.

There are several less than adequate approaches to Carbohydrate Loading, but the general formats are similar. Here is a typical poor example. Such approaches work, but not as well as they should.

For a marathon on Saturday, you begin the previous Sunday. Sunday, Monday and Tuesday you run extremely long distances (20, 15, 12 miles) and eat a diet low in carbohydrates and high in fat and protein. Wednesday you run as far as you can.

Wednesday through Friday you stuff yourself with every kind of high carbohydrate yuck you can get into your gob and Friday night before the race you have a *big spaghetti dinner* and lots of sweet dessert. Put honey on everything.

Saturday morning you get up a couple of hours before the race and, if you wish, have a carbohydrate breakfast—and you're fixed. I'll say you're *fixed!* Don't Do It!, Don't Do It! and I repeat *DON'T DO IT!!!*

135

The Perfect Marathon — Part II

The only thing correct in the above diet is that it begins on Sunday. Ignore the rest. We want to avoid (as much as possible) upsetting the digestive system (with all that yuck) and we want to avoid exhausting the body so near race time with excessively long runs. We do want to deplete glycogen and we do want to pack it in. First a warning.

If you have hypoglycemia this is NOT for you. If you have any food allergies or special tastes in foods, change the diet to suit yourself. If you have digestive problems check with your doctor before you try this diet.

Since I thrive on a low carbohydrate diet, I have never had ill effects from loading. One friend who seems to be a borderline hypoglycemic practically freaked out on the second day. So he ran down to the store and ate a half-gallon of ice cream.

Now to the *Schreiber Carbohydrate Loading System*. Since loading causes some people to gain weight, we begin our diet several weeks before anyone else. Begin cutting a little on food intake, especially in the area of fat and oil.

If you've already decided what you want to weigh for the race, try to get to that weight—or a couple of pounds lighter—two weeks before the big day.

Presuming that the marathon is to be on a Saturday morning, begin the previous Sunday morning with a slow run of from 10 to 15 miles, depending on your state of training. If your week's total is from 50 to 60 miles and you run an 18 or 20-miler every week, a 10-12 mile depletion run should be long enough. If you are a little better trained, run 12-15 miles.

This Sunday's run is not training. It is too late to train. All you want to do is use up glycogen. Run at a very comfortable pace. Enjoy yourself. Stop to stretch whenever you feel like it.

After this Sunday depletion run you are effectively off carbohydrates . . .but what are you on?

You'll be able to eat just about anything; just no bread, potatoes, pasta, beans, fruit and stuff like that.

Here's what I eat for the next three days. You can follow it or just use it for a guideline.

Tomatoes (a small one each day); lettuce (1/3 head each day); chicken livers (one pound divided over the three days); boiled chicken (as much as I feel like—or as little); Super Yeast (at least two tablespoons in soup); Vitamin C (4 grams a day as a powder—drink lots of water); Vitamin E (1000 IU taken with food but not at the same meal as the Vitamin C); crude bran (two or three tablespoons a day in water); cheese (as a snack if desired); and plain/natural yogurt (as needed, but no more than a ½ pint per day).

One of the problems you may face during the depletion phase of this diet is the almost uncontrollable desire to stuff yourself with french fries and cream cakes. When you *first* get that *hint of desire*, try taking a heaping teaspoon of plain yogurt. When and if it gets rough, you can take a teaspoon of yogurt every half hour—anything to keep from blowing the works.

The *first day of the depletion you jogged between 10 and 15 miles. On Monday take a slow run of 5 to 7 miles*. Again, this depends on your state of training. Since this is probably much less than you are used to, throw in some extra stretching exercises during the day.

I sometimes do 15 or 20 minutes on an exercise bicycle and some lightweight leg curls and extensions on a weight machine. (Be sure to allow 5 to 8 hours between using a leg machine and running.) Since I do these exercises slowly and with little weight, I get no cardiovascular benefit, but they are enough to help further reduce glycogen stores in my leg muscles—and it saves my feet, ankles, knees and hips.

Tuesday is the same as Monday except I only run 5 miles.

Wednesday morning is your big day . . .what you've been waiting for. Get up early and run *5 miles . . .if you can*. It may be very difficult. You will be heavy-legged and crabby and your mouth will feel like the entire Russian army marched through it in their sweat socks. Gut it out even if you have to stop and walk a couple of times, because you are about to be rewarded. After this morning's run is BREAKFAST . . .but I must warn you again. If you are hypoglycemic, this is NOT for you.

Breakfast is pancakes and/or waffles drenched in MAGIC SUPERPOWERED MAPLE SYRUP*, small hamburger patty or a piece of cheese, half a grapefruit or grapefruit juice, and coffee, tea or milk.

Lunch is one or more peanut butter/wheat germ** sandwiches on whole wheat bread, vegetables, fruit, plus whatever else you want as long as it is low in fat and has no added sugar.

Supper should be based around pasta or rice and bread. Potatoes are also good. Be sure to include vegetables, fruit and some protein, and avoid things with refined sugar. Also, no honey.

The most important meals during the carbohydrate loading stage are the first meal after depletion and those eaten within 8 hours. From then on, you must keep the carbohydrate intake up, but you must also guard against overeating.

Keep intake of all fats low, eat nothing with added sugar. Get your carbohydrates from grain, rice, bread, potatoes, pasta and the like. Get your protein from lean beef, boiled chicken, non-oily fish, uncreamed cottage cheese, lowfat plain yogurt, natural peanut butter with the oil skimmed off, and wheat germ. Eat mixed salads and cooked greens without dressing (except lemon juice). Use the same vitamins and supplements suggested in the weight loss diet. *STAY AWAY FROM BEANS AND PEAS* or you may be inviting some gut-rumble problems. Some people may have trouble digesting wheat. If you're one of them substitute rice, potatoes and the other root vegetables.

Thursday morning run 2 or 3 miles, depending on how you feel. *Friday don't run at all.*

Friday night's meal is the most misunderstood of all. It is important that it be small. I generally have a small plate of spaghetti and mushroom sauce (no meat), a small salad, several pieces of bread and a small glass of wine. Frank Shorter drinks beer.

---

*MAGIC SUPERPOWERED MAPLE SYRUP: Use the recipe on the side of *Adams Maple Flavor Extract* EXCEPT instead of sugar USE FRUCTOSE and use twice as much as suggested in the recipe for sugar. (Fructose is available in health food stores. It should be used only for this first meal. Not for hypoglycemics!)

**PEANUT BUTTER/WHEAT GERM: Skim the oil from a jar of natural peanut butter and set aside. Add one-third wheat germ to two-thirds peanut butter with oil removed and mix well.

The Perfect Marathon — Part II

Saturday, marathon day, if the race is to be at 8 or 9 I get up at 5 or 6 a.m. and slowly eat a small banana and drink a small can of unsweetened grapefruit juice. Ralph used to eat several bite-sized candy bars along with his banana. I wouldn't, but each one of us has to pick his own poison.

The above *timetable* of depletion and loading works well for me; however, if you begin experiencing extra heavy urination on Friday afternoon, it probably means your body is beginning to dump glycogen. If this *is* the case with you, next time begin your depletion on Sunday evening instead of morning and do your final depletion run and first packing session Wednesday evening instead of morning.

As you gain more experience with depletion/packing and learn to read your own body, you will be able to refine the system to meet your own needs.

What we are trying to do is get the most depletion without hurting the body; and the most packing without undue weight gain. Try to arrive at the starting line with a calm gut.

Some runners, the cautious ones, go through a test depletion and packing several months before a race just to see what it's like and to get their timing down. Others figure it's going to be so bad they can't imagine doing it more than once, so they wait until race week.

I was one of the cautious ones and did a test depletion. I didn't find it much different from my regular diet. When I did it for race week the first time it still wasn't difficult. The only problem I had was a slight feeling of depression and a great weariness during my Wednesday morning run—but breakfast fixed that!

I wouldn't go into a marathon without doing the entire depletion/packing diet. Some top runners feel the same way. Other top-ranking marathoners shun the whole idea and many use only the packing stage. Like everything else, the final decision is up to you.

Chapter VI
Superpowered Drinks
Training - Electrolytic Replacement - Post Race Recovery

By now, you probably sense that *I Love To Eat!* Matter of fact, there are many times that I'd rather stuff myself with roast goose and plum dressing than run. The thing is, after running I feel great and after stuffing myself I feel, well . . .stuffed. A difficult situation.

Not only do I love to eat, but I love to cook as well. The compromise forced upon me is the same as my compromise with ice cream. During the week I do right by my body, and on the weekends I pig-out. I know you will be disappointed, but this little essay is not going to be about the gluttonous weekends. Alas . . .it will be about the virtuous weekdays.

About ten or fifteen years ago when I was trying to kick a milk shake habit, I began dreaming up varius drinks and liquid meals to be made in a blender. I wanted things that wouldn't take long to prepare, would taste good, leave me refreshed and wouldn't pack on the blubber. If they turned out to be nutritious, that would be an added bonus. I collected that bonus.

Some of my creations are too far-out even for this book, but here are the ones that managed (if just barely) to pass the test of sanity. I've divided them into three categories: *training, replacement and recovery*. Of course, you can use them anytime you want.

In a few cases I have included unadulterated items because I feel they are wonderful in themselves—like ice water.

Training Drinks Perhaps it is cultural, but many of my meals and drinks are based upon a simple clear soup stock, usually chicken. The soup can be eaten hot, cold and as a jelly. It can be mixed with many other foods and is ideal for the liquid in which to cook greens, boil potatoes, simmer squash, etc.

139

The Perfect Marathon — Part II

The basic stock is very easy to prepare. *Simmer* chicken, turkey parts or beef short ribs all day in water with a touch of lemon juice, white wine or vinegar. Add no seasonings; that comes later.

Remove all solids—meat, bones, etc.—and chill the liquid overnight. In the morning skim off the fat, leaving a thick jelly. If the stock is not jelled, simmer awhile longer and chill again. Make at least a quart.

One of my favorite ways of using the broth, especially on a cold winter evening, is to combine two cups of jelled broth, a tablespoon of lemon juice and Light Salt to taste. Simmer in a saucepan. Cream a rounded tablespoon of Super Yeast (with added calcium and magnesium) with two or three tablespoons of the warm broth mixture and add to the contents of the saucepan. Bring to a rolling boil. Dribble in two previously beaten eggs. Dribble the eggs slowly or they will congeal instead of mixing. Stir swiftly for a few seconds with a fork and remove from the heat. Season with salt, pepper and chopped scallions or chives. Serve immediately.

Now, here's my plan to kick the milk shake habit. If you like ice cream, this is for you. Not only does it taste wonderful, but it is good for you and has a fraction of the calories of the real thing.

Pour eight ounces of cold milk into a chilled blender. Add half a cup of instant nonfat powdered milk, one broken-up banana, two fresh whole eggs, a cap or two of vanilla extract, a packet of diet sweetener, a pinch of Light Salt, and a level teaspoon of Super Yeast. Gradually work up to two heaping tablespoons of yeast as you learn to enjoy the flavor. Beat at a low/medium speed until completely blended. Chill in the freezer. Loosen any frozen crust that may have formed and beat again only for a few seconds. Pour this wonderful stuff into a frosted crystal goblet and garnish with a sprig of mint. If you don't have a frosted goblet, drink it right out of the frosty blender.

Here's another cold drink that's faster to make than the previous one and, lo and behold, it's a complete meal-in-a-glass.

Into a blender place one cup of whole milk, half a cup of natural yogurt, a quarter-cup of wheat germ, two fresh whole eggs, any nice fruit you have around, a pinch of Light Salt, some Super Yeast and, if you like, diet sweetener or honey to taste. Add five or six *crushed* ice cubes and blend only until completely mixed. I enjoy this so much that I have been known to keep drinking it until I'm too bloated to move . . .well, almost.

Enough cold stuff for awhile. Let's warm up. The following is something of a variation on the first recipe and uses my old favorite, V-8 Juice.

Into a saucepan place one cup of V-8 Juice, one cup of jelled broth, a teaspoon of lemon juice, Super Yeast (see previous recipes) and salt and pepper to taste. Bring slowly to a rolling boil and dribble in two previously beaten eggs. Remove from the heat, stir with a fork for a few seconds and serve—with garlic toast. Yum!

Electrolytic Replacement Drinks It all began when someone tried to help out a bunch of suffering football players by inventing salty pop. Since then any number of companies and individuals have been marketing concoctions designed to refresh athletes. Basically these products are sugared water with a few minerals and some coloring. For the most part they are not nearly as helpful as plain water because the sugar hinders absorption from the stomach. In addition, some tests have shown that most of these drinks include minerals which are not really needed, and lack other minerals normally lost in perspiration. There are a few exceptions.

Two commercial replacement drinks that I like are Body Punch and ERG/Gooknaid (Electrolytic Replacement with Glucose). ERG was invented by Mr. Gookin, who analyzed his own sweat and attempted to recreate its mineral content.

I never use a replacement drink during a marathon, but a large percentage of runners do. I just feel better with water. I have used Body Punch and ERG after workouts on hot days (when no beer or Coke was available), and Linda Lindsey, the nurturer mentioned earlier, fed me a quart of Body Punch one brutal afternoon when I was helping her mow the lawn. It was a first class refresher.

The worst thing about some of the more popular athletic drinks is that they have a tremendous amount of sugar. This isn't so bad under mild running conditions, but it is totally unacceptable under

ELECTROLYTIC REPLACEMENT DRINKS

marathon conditions when the water must get out of the stomach into the system. This supersweet stuff makes many runners sick, me included.

ERG has one of the lowest sugar contents of any of the commercial preparations. Perrier has no sugar at all and none of the crud often found in tap water. It's simply a lot of H_2O and a good supply of minerals.

Regardless of what you finally decide to drink, test it out and make sure it doesn't do funny things to your system. If there is a special concoction that suits you or that you feel lucky with, you'll have to arrange to get it from a friend. Many runners have friends following them on bicycles, handing out cold drinks and cool washcloths. Nice if you can get it . . .but some race directors say no.

If you really want to make up your own replacement drink (I still like plain cold water) begin with boiled or filtered tap water, bottled spring water, or bottled distilled water. Warm it up. To this tepid water add a small amount of Light Salt and maybe a little glucose and/or fructose. The actual amounts can be arrived at by tasting. When you can *just barely detect* the presence of salt and sweet, you have too much . . .add a cup of water. Chill the mixture and put it up in half-pint bottles. During a marathon these bottles should be kept on ice. If you can arrange it, have someone hand you a bottle every two or three miles for the first sixteen to eighteen miles. No, I don't expect you to run the last eight miles with half a dozen or more plastic bottles in your arms. Have your friend take back each bottle as soon as you are refreshed.

Since water empties from the stomach faster when it is cool, you should drink your mixture at a temperature of 40°–50°F. No need for a thermometer. If it feels cool, it is cool.

I must repeat that the various replacement drinks, including the one above, are only for people who really believe they need them. I think you are much better off with cold water.

Although many runners would agree that water is the best beverage during a marathon, many other runners, and top ones at that, would strongly disagree. Many will drink anything that's offered, as long as it's wet. Others have their particular favorites. I think the following idea is revolting, but at least one elite marathoner thrives on it: allow a quart of Coke to go flat and drink it warm during the race. Maybe it would be improved if it were taken chilled, but I doubt it. Definitely not for me—maybe for you?

Here's a good one for short training runs during hot weather. Be sure to try it out first before you attempt to use it for a long run. Cut unsweetened grapefruit juice with three parts of water. Add an optional pinch of Light Salt. Chill. Always shake before using. Some athletes thrive on this, others urp.

141

The Perfect Marathon — Part II

I've seen many marathoners drink beer late in a race and they seem to get a kick from it. When I've tried beer during a marathon, the stuff foamed, went up to my nose and gave me a pain in the chest—from gas I guess. Although the pain went away in a couple of minutes, I don't think I'll try it again.

A year or so ago I read about another alcohol trick. The procedure, as I remember it, was to have someone hand you a cup of very cold water laced with a shot of vodka. I think you're supposed to down the ice-dynamite at the eighteen-mile mark. Theoretically the alcohol is metabolized immediately and used as fuel, never having the chance to reach the brain. The lift, at least according to theory, is almost instantaneous, and the jolt forward quite satisfying. I haven't tried it yet and I don't advise it, but it is interesting.

So far I've just given you drinks, or at least liquids. I am going to digress for a moment to an interesting form of hypochondria that strikes many first-time marathoners. It is the "I Am Going To Starve To Death" syndrome.

For some reason a lot of people think they are going to perish from starvation during the two-and-a-half to five-and-a-half hours spent running the twenty-six miles three hundred and eighty-five yards. Believe me. You're not going to starve.

A friend who was once a beginning marathoner and now is an ultra and super ultra-marathoner (races of fifty to one hundred miles), went to his first race worrying about starvation or malnutrition, or something. He had his wife make him a special bag to tie around his waist. Into this he poured a variety of candy bars, hard candies, chocolate kisses, jelly beans—you name it. Can you imagine how sick he was by the halfway mark? You can't possibly imagine! He was so sick . . .oh, why go on? It was terrible!

Post Race Recovery Drinks For the final minute or two of a marathon and for some seconds thereafter the mind and senses are wide open, sucking everything in. A short while later the brain shuts off. Like a spawning salmon or a migrating lemming, the marathoner at the end of a race has become a monomaniac. The one overpowering desire is to get as wet as possible (inside) as soon as possible. They'll take whatever you give them, as long as it comes soon, cold and in great volume.

I don't always have a choice, but my four personal favorites are: a quart of Coke over crushed ice; very dark beer; Perrier over crushed ice; apple juice over crushed ice. Whichever you hand me first I'll take, and love.

Once I get back to the hotel or home, I like to have one part ice cream, one part natural yogurt, two parts milk and a pinch of Light Salt all beaten together in a blender. To make it even more fantastic I sometimes substitute peach yogurt ice cream for the regular ice cream.

POST RACE RECOVERY DRINKS

If you plan to stay out at the race site for an afternoon picnic, here's a refresher you can make right there—providing you have had the foresight to pack an ice chest. I have been known to drink a quart of this in a single pour down my gullet. Mix one part of very cold Coke with one part of very cold milk. I know how it sounds, but it tastes out-of-this-world.

Here's another one that sounds strange but goes down refreshingly smooth. For about two weeks last summer I drank a quart of this stuff after every hot run. Mix three parts of chilled unsweetened pink grapefruit juice with one part chilled Coke or Tab. Add a squeeze of lemon juice and an optional pinch of Light Salt.

For a continental touch mix one part of jelled broth with two parts ice water. Add a squeeze of lemon or lime, a pinch of Light Salt and pepper—Worcestershire sauce too, if you like. Shake well and serve cold. Like most of my concoctions this one is 400% more delicious than it sounds. If you add a little something extra this makes a delightful cocktail for the post race orgies—and it's good for you.

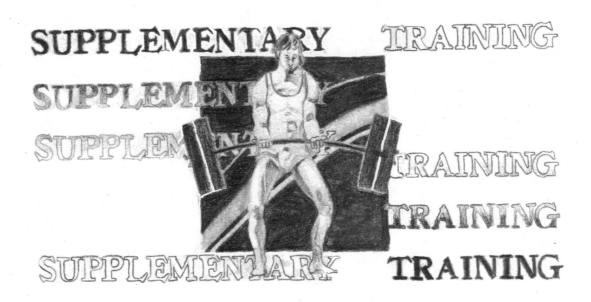

Chapter VII
A Weighty Discussion

There is probably no other sport in the United States that has received such *bad press* over the years as weight training. A perfect example is a meaningless term that always seems to appear when the subject of resistance training, weight lifting or bodybuilding is written about or mentioned. Here it comes again: muscle-bound.

I gather that muscle-bound is supposed to mean that anyone who develops their body to Grecian proportions or who takes to the barbells is somehow going to be so bound up by their own muscles that they will be practically immobilized.

It is true that *improper* application of almost any training can result in restricted range of movement (observe the hamstrings of many distance runners). However the proper use of weights can actually enhance flexibility.

Over the past 20 years more and more Olympic-class athletes in a wide variety of sports, but particularly in track-and-field and swimming, have been using weights as part of their training routines. I have even heard tell of ballet and modern dancers who use weights—What does that do to the muscle-binding theory!

Not surprisingly, marathoners seemed to have stayed away from the weights. In the marathon a premium is placed on low body weight, and barbells have the reputation for packing on bulk—something a distance runner doesn't need.

It is true that body builders pack on considerable weight, but it doesn't come easy. The amount of lifting they have to do and the enormous meals they have to eat in order to gain that bulk is positively staggering. A distance runner who uses resistance training as an *adjunct* to running has little to worry about and much to gain.

"OK, so pumping iron won't necessarily bind me up, flesh me out or slow me down. But what will it do to make me a better runner?"

For starters, running strengthens and shortens muscles such as the hamstrings (the leg biceps) creating a potential imbalance with the quadriceps (muscles on the front of the leg above the knee). Strength imbalances between opposing muscles groups greatly increase the chances of injury.

Weight training can help correct problems of imbalance before you pull a muscle. Begin by carefully stretching both the hamstrings and the quadriceps. One step further and we get to leg extensions and leg curls. For this one you'll need one or more of the following: access to a leg curl machine (health club?), a pair of iron shoes or leg weights. Leg weights weigh between one and five pounds.

When you first start you must use ridiculously light weights and very few repetitions. I have no idea of your capacity, but one pound and five repetitions is not too easy. Bit by bit you will do more repetitions until you reach twenty or so; then you add a little more weight. As you get used to these exercises you will probably be using different weights for the curls and extensions because the hamstrings and quadriceps have different relative strengths.

Leg extensions are executed while seated on the edge of a high bench or table, which should be high enough so your feet barely touch the floor. Alternating left and right, raise your lower leg straight out in front of you, then let it back down—under control. The movement should be smooth and relatively slow.

Leg curls are executed while lying face down on a bench. The legs are alternately *curled* until the heel closely approaches the buttocks. Don't curl so tightly that a cramp results. The movement should be comfortable.

Because the goal of the distance runner is to keep body weight low, burn up fat and increase strength and endurance, our methodology will be different from the sprinter who wants to build explosive strength, or the bodybuilder who wants to build massive but defined bulk.

The usual procedure in bodybuilding is to perform a movement six to ten times. Each movement is called a rep. The group of six to ten movements is called a set. A "standard" routine will often consist of three sets of six reps each using maximum weight.

After several workouts at this level, the number of reps is increased by one. When the routine finally arrives at three sets of ten reps the weight is increased and the reps reduced back to six . . .and it all begins again. With this system one uses a weight that is relatively easy to move at the beginning of the set, but nearly impossible to move by the last rep. In fact, by the last rep of the last set it may be necessary to get outside help to finish the exercise. The approach will build impressive musculature and very impressive short-duration strength.

While our approach will be different from the bodybuilder's, it will not be *that* different. The only thing we really change is the number of reps. All the other rules of good weight training remain the same: no swinging and cheating, full movements from extensions to contraction, and no sitting around talking instead of doing.

Weight training, like beginning jogging, takes some getting used to. When you started jogging you got into it first by walking and then graduated to very short and easy runs. When you first begin with the weights you start *very* light and with few repetitions/reps. At first the weight will *seem* too light, but don't be fooled. The results of imprudent resistance training are the same with running: sore tendons, strained muscles and an interrupted jogging schedule.

With leg extensions and curls, pick a weight you can use comfortably for one set of five reps, then work up slowly through Chart One in this section. Continue or even increase your stretching.

Don't get up. Since you are sitting on the edge of the bench, legs dangling, might as well tackle the alternating toe raise (no relation to the Yellow Bellied Purse Snatcher).

145

The Perfect Marathon — Part II

When doing the toe raise all pivoting is done at the ankle joint, and the exercise attacks the complex of muscles at the front of the lower leg.

Drape a purse, bean bag, ankle weight—whatever—over your foot. Drop your toes as low as they will go, stretching the lower leg muscles—the weight will slide off your foot. Put it back on again. Now raise your toes/foot (pivoting only at the ankle) as high as you can, contracting the lower leg muscles. Repeat only a few times with each foot at first. Add a few reps every once in a while.

As in any sport there is always the danger that things will get out of hand. In car racing you keep wanting to go faster. In distance training mileage keeps increasing if you let it. In weight training there are always more reps, more sets and greater poundage.

If you decide to stop and hold at this point with the leg exercises, they will certainly be a plus factor in your training. If you do have the time and inclination to go just a bit further, I think you will find yourself amply rewarded.

A moment's digression. I have yet to make a distinction between training methods for men and methods for women. I still am not going to make such a distinction. I believe that *men as a group* and *women as a group* can use the same methodology. The only differences that come to mind are individual, and would cross sexual boundaries.

The reason I bring the point up at this time is that many women are reticent about training with weights. I am sure there are many reasons for this, but the one most verbalized is a fear of developing large muscles. Forget it. Muscles are very difficult to develop and most men who go to gyms to achieve the MR. AMERICA LOOK rarely get more than a small bump on their arms.

The effort required to develop imposing biceps (not good, not bad, just very large) is excessive almost beyond belief.

Quite a number of years ago I was working out in a gym where there were several men training for the Mr. California contest. The physical effort and mental concentration that they put into a final set of arm curls or leg

KNEE UPS

presses was the equivalent of running the last one hundred yards of a marathon a half dozen times in succession.

The point to all this, ladies *and* gentlemen: this program is not going to turn you into a muscle-person, but it can give you a real edge in the marathon when the going gets rough.

Switching to an advanced endurance schedule requires three sets of twenty-two, working up to three sets of thirty, and over to two sets of thirty-five.

Continuing with this progression you eventually arrive at a couple of sets of forty or fifty or a single set of seventy-five to a hundred. When you arrive at this elite level you can vary your workouts depending on how you feel that day.

Presumably, throughout this entire process you have been using the same weight that you used for the original two sets of ten reps. If you find at any time during the schedule that this weight has become too heavy, use a lighter weight. If it's too light, use more poundage—naturally.

What you want is to be able to do a hell-of-a-lot-of reps with just enough weight to give you a feeling of resistance. At the end of the session you should feel tired in the legs and mind, but not strained.

If you're serious about using this system, work the legs no more and no less than three times per week. If you work out the legs on the same days that you run, allow *a minimum of 5 hours of rest* between weight work on the legs and running . . .*8 hours would be better*.

If you don't allow ample time between running and working the legs with weights, you *will* pull a muscle . . .I guarantee this from personal experience. Another warning. Don't work the legs with weights on the same day you do your long run—do so and you will discover yet another sure way of pulling muscles.

The charts that follow, like all charts in the book, are not rigid. They are intended to provide a framework on which to build your own training structure. You may, of course, use them as presented or amend them to suit your own needs and natural abilities.

Because we do not wish to increase visible muscle mass, the weight you use remains fairly constant. The work load increases through the imaginative use of reps and sets. By messing about with these two variables you can get a nice progression without wracking yourself up, and putting a big, unplanned gap in your training schedule.

CHART ONE
Set and Rep Progression for Hamstring and Quadricep Endurance

# =	very light weight	++# =	still sort of light, not that light
+# =	not quite so light		

Rep/Set   Use the same progression for Leg Extensions and Leg Curls

Week	Monday	Wednesday	Friday
1.	# 5/1	# 6/1	# 7/1
2.	# 8/1	# 9/1	#10/1
3.	#12/1	#14/1	#16/1
4.	#18/1	#20/1	#20/1
5.	+#10/1	+#12/1	+#14/1
6.	+#16/1	+#18/1	+#20/1
7.	++#15/1	++#18/1	++#20/1
8.	++#10/2	++#12/2	++#15/2

The weight you use should be enough to tire you by the end of the session, but you shouldn't have to strain. Alternate curls and extensions. When you have two sets of each it should look like this: ten leg curls/ten extensions/ten curls/ten extensions

CHART TWO
Set and Rep Progression for Hamstring and Quadricep Endurance

M =   light to moderate weight

Rep/Set

Week	Monday	Wednesday	Friday
1.	M 10/2	M 11/2	M 12/2
2.	M 6/3	M 7/3	M 8/3
3.	M 9/3	M 10/3	M 10/3
4.	M 15/2	M 16/2	M 18/2
5.	M 20/2	M 20/2	M 20/2
6.	M 14/3	M 16/3	M 17/3
7.	M 18/3	M 20/3	M 20/3
8.	M 25/2	M 28/2	M 30/2

CHART THREE
Advanced Endurance Weight Training—Hamstrings and Quadriceps

M =   light to moderate weight

Rep/Set

Week	Monday	Wednesday	Friday
1.	M 22/3	M 24/3	M 26/3
2.	M 28/3	M 30/3	M 30/3
3.	M 35/2	M 38/2	M 40/2
4.	M 40/2	M 50/1	M 55/1
5.	M 60/1	M 65/1	M 70/1
6.	M 50/2	M 55/2	M 60/2
7.	M 60/2	M 75/1	M 75/1
8.	M 65/2	M 80/1	M 65/2

And on and on and on . . .

The leg curls and extensions are primarily muscle exercises and have little or no effect on the cardiovascular system . . . which brings up a pet peeve of mine.

In many books on running I have seen an oft-repeated theme. The statement usually is that working out with weights is an anaerobic activity rather than an aerobic activity. This idea comes from confusing *weight lifting* with *weight training*.

Competitive weight lifting requires massive expenditures of energy over extremely brief periods of time, much as in running dashes. However, no track coach would say the running per se is anaerobic just because the hundred-yard dash is anaerobic.

Discounting weight lifting and concentrating only on weight training, it is possible to do both aerobic and anaerobic exercises. The leg curls and extensions we've just covered fit into neither category—at least for training purposes. The exertion is not difficult enough or prolonged enough to cause oxygen debt and the heart rate is not elevated enough to allow for aerobic conditioning. The next exercise is definitely aerobic. In fact, it is the one I use to maintain fitness when I'm injured (knock on wood).

Early in my premarathon training I was injured frequently due to imprudence and overzealousness. The exercise that saved me was the half squat—also known as the partial deep knee bend.

This exercise can be performed using body weight as resistance, dumbbells in the hands, a barbell across the shoulders or even a backpack filled with books. I've used all these methods and others depending on the results I was looking for. In most cases though, I believe distance runners would do best using only body weight.

The only piece of equipment you'll need is a four-foot length of 2x4 or anything that will elevate your heels a couple of inches. When I do these at the track I sometimes put my heels up on the edge of the shot put ring, but that's a little high. Better is the coping that goes around the track itself.

Heels elevated, squat down until your thighs and lower legs are at about a 45° angle to each other. Now come back up to an erect position. If you wish you can go down a little farther until your upper leg is parallel to the ground, but that's as far as you should go. You want to guard against stretching the ligaments of your knee. If you're using heavy weights, if you go down too far, or if you use a bouncing motion, the risk of knee injury is greatly amplified.

If you're doing your partial squats at home there's a trick I learned years ago that will definitely take the strain off your knees. Back up to a high padded bench. Squat until your butt just touches the bench, then stand smoothly erect.

Now I certainly won't say that partial squats are as effective for aerobic conditioning as jogging and running; what is? However, by picking the proper speed and without using additional weight I can get my pulse up to 120 beats per minute and hold it there for half an hour and longer.

At the track extra weights are more or less out of the question; I just couldn't see lugging all that junk around. When working out at the gym or in my home gym, I've done squats with dumbbells in my hands and a barbell across my shoulders—but not at the same time forgodsakes! These two ways of adding extra weight work fine for *short sessions*. As for long sessions, I don't even like to think about holding a pair of dumbbells until my fingers turn to quivering jelly. A barbell is no better. After a very few minutes of supporting a bar across my shoulders, the muscles begin to cramp and my neckbone gets sore. Sets of 30 or 40, or even a few more, are okay. But for me at least, a half hour holding a barbell or a pair of dumbbells is out of the question.

The most comfortable way I have found of adding resistance to partial squats is to use one of those lightweight canvas bags that cyclists wear to carry books and stuff. If you want to add even more weight you can use a hard frame backpack. I've used one with as much as 75 pounds in it.

Bodybuilders and other weight trainers will scoff at the idea of squatting with 75 pounds—they use hundreds. However, I am talking about using up to 75 pounds for doing continuous squats for half an hour or longer.

Perhaps continuous isn't quite accurate. I often stop in the upright position for as long as five or six seconds and sometimes *shake out my legs* before continuing. I might do this every few minutes after the first ten or fifteen minutes.

The Perfect Marathon — Part II

If you do begin using partial squats in your training, definitely *start without weight* and start with a very few repetitions. This exercise will work great if you never add any poundage—but some folks like to punish themselves.

The following chart is a basic conditioning progression. Normally the progression would be much faster; this chart, however, is designed to avoid as much as possible any soreness that might interrupt running.

Male or female, those thigh and butt muscles are big, heavy, strong and important hunks of meat. They can do a tremendous amount of work. You can go right out the first day and do some pretty impressive squats, either in terms of weight or time/reps. A few hours later and for many days to come, you may be too sore to tie your shoes. I've gotten so sore from overdoing squats that I had to use my hand to lift my foot off the gas pedal onto the brake.

CHART ONE
Half (Partial) Squats for Added Leg Endurance

Rep/Set

A Rep is a single complete movement in an exercise. A Set is a group of such movements. Example: Do ten squats. You have done 10 Reps. If you do no more, you have done one Set of 10 Reps (10/1). If you do another ten, you have done two Sets of 10 Reps (10/2).

Week	Monday	Tuesday	Wednesday	Thursday	Friday
1.	2/2	3/2	4/2	5/2	6/2
2.	5/3	6/3	7/3	8/3	9/3
3.	10/3	12/2	14/2	16/2	18/2
4.	20/2	15/3	16/3	18/3	20/3
5.	22/3	25/3	30/2	35/2	40/2
6.	40/2	45/2	55/1	60/1	65/1
7.	65/1	70/1	75/1	80/1	85/1
8.	90/1	90/1	95/1	95/1	100/1

Continue at a level of from 75 to 100/1.

Squats should be performed with the heels slightly elevated (1½''–2''). Use no additional weight at first. Squat down only until the upper and lower legs make a 45° angle. Do not bounce or put undue stress on the knees. Do not pause in the squatting position; come immediately and smoothly erect at the end of the exercise.

As a supplement to running, partial squats are one of the best exercises on the list. As an alternative exercise when you are prevented from jogging at all, it's still hard to beat the partial squat. Chart Two is a fairly advanced routine so be sure to work through the first chart before you attempt this more strenuous version.

CHART TWO
Half (Partial) Squats as a Short Term Alternate to Jogging

Week	Minutes Morning/Minutes Evening						
	Sun.	Mon.	Tues.	Wed.	Thurs.	Fri.	Sat.
1.	10/10	12/12	14/14	15/15	15/15	12/17	12/19
2.	15/20	15/25	12/30	0/35	0/40	0/45	0/45

. . .and continue at the 35 to 45 minute level until you are able to run again, then switch back to Chart One on a three day per week basis.

150

When using partial squats as a temporary subsitute for jogging, don't start counting time until after your pulse has risen to 120 beats per minute. Check your pulse for 10 seconds. Around 20 beats or more is a go and you can start marking time. It can take quite some time to get your pulse up to a *working level,* so you might start out doing the exercise fairly rapidly, then taper off to a somewhat slower pace. If you are in exceptionally good condition, with a resting pulse in the 30s and low 40s, you may never be able to get your rate up to 120 via squats. In that case just get it as high as you can and make do.

Running obviously requires strong legs. Not quite so obviously, it also requires a strong stomach, back, chest, shoulders and arms.

You're going to have to hold up your arms for 26.2 miles and those arms are going to be moving back and forth at the exact same pace as your legs . . .they will get tired and so will the rest of your body from the hips on up. When I was running in my first marathon my right side got so tired I was dragging my arm and shoulder like Igor from the Frankenstein movies.

Earlier in this section I pointed out that resistance training is as important for women as for men. Now that we are at the hips and working up, I'd like to modify that statement. I would like it to read that resistance training is at least as important for women as for men.

Over the past couple of years large numbers of women have been applying as police and fire department cadets. Most of them have been immediately washed out because of the poor upper body strength.

Generally speaking, there have been two knee-jerk reactions to women being washed-out of training classes on the basis of physical tests: first, that women are just naturally weak in the upper body (bullfeathers!) and second, that these tests are somehow unfair to women (double-bull). I know of one woman in particular who did get in and graduated. She simply went out for two months before she applied and practiced doing chins from a bar . . .same as the guys did (but she hadn't told anyone).

Woman or man, if you lack strength in some part of your body, exercise and you will get stronger. For whatever reason, many women have not engaged in activities that promote upper body strength . . .now we will change that.

If you don't give a damn how you look, these exercises will help make you a better runner and a better athlete in general. If you do give a damn how you look, these exercises will make you look better and still improve your running.

Let's start with the gut. Sit-ups with bent knees are a resistance exercise using the weight of the upper body. If you use a slant board the resistance can be changed by changing the angle of incline. You can also add resistance by holding a book, a heavy purse or a barbell plate on the chest or behind the head.

No need to tell you to go easy on these at first . . .you've already had plentyof experience doing bent knee sit-ups morning and evening since you started jogging.

A variation on the sit-up is the *supine leg-raise.* Lie flat on your back and lift both legs together. Don't raise your head or upper body at the same time as your raise your legs; this can put too much strain on your lower back.

I have a bad back, so after awhile sit-ups start to bother me. I prefer *knee-ups from a chinning bar.* Hanging from an overhead bar I draw my knees slowly toward my chest, then lower them to the full hanging position . . .but you've also been doing these right along—haven't you? To add resistance to the knee-ups I wear ankle weights of from 1½ to 2 pounds each . . .not much, but enough.

The main limiting factor when doing the bar exercises is not the strength of your stomach or even your legs. It's your hands that will do you in. Chalk will help keep tired hands from slipping and frequent short rests between sets will delay the point when your hands finally refuse to cling to the bar. Over time your hands and forearms will get a great deal stronger and so will your stomach and leg muscles. Once you get the reps up, the hands will still go before the stomach.

The Perfect Marathon — Part II

Sit-ups exercise mainly the upper rectus abdominis while knee-ups and supine leg-raises get to the lower. The rectus abdominis are those washboard-like muscles on the front of your stomach (if you are strong *and* skinny). The rope-like muscles along the sides of your stomach are the internal and external obliques. You can get to these by hanging from a bar, legs together and drawing up your body, first to one side and then to the other.

This is a little difficult to understand at first, so think of yourself as a dangling puppet. There are strings coming out of the *sides* of your thighs between the knee and the hip. The puppet master first draws up on the right string, holds it, lets it down and then draws up on the left string. Just a little practice is all it takes.

Standing *side-bends* with a very light weight (a book?) in each hand will effect the obliques and so will twisting sit-ups.

The twisting *sit-up* is performed with the knees bent and the hands behind the head, elbows out. As you come up touch your right knee with the left elbow. The next time touch your left knee with the right elbow and continue alternating.

Another extremely effective exercise for these muscles at the waist is the *lateral leg-raise*. Lie on your right side and lift your left leg as high as it will go. Do this for x number of Reps and switch to your left side, raising your right leg as high as it will go.

Unlike most of the other exercises, lateral leg-raises offer almost no resistance on their own—especially to the trained runner. It is possible to do sit-ups, knee-ups from a bar and leg-raises (lying flat on your back) without additional weight and still get a good workout. Lateral leg-raises, on the other hand, are little more than easy calisthenics. Add a pound or two of ankle weight and—Zowie—they become *real* exercise.

After long preparation some weight trainers use iron shoes when doing lateral raises (lying on the side or standing). These iron shoes can weigh up to five pounds, plus another five pounds if a solid iron dumbbell bar is attached. The attached bar will accept standard weight discs so it is quite easy to load an iron shoe up to fifty pounds, if you can use iron weights, not plastic ones.

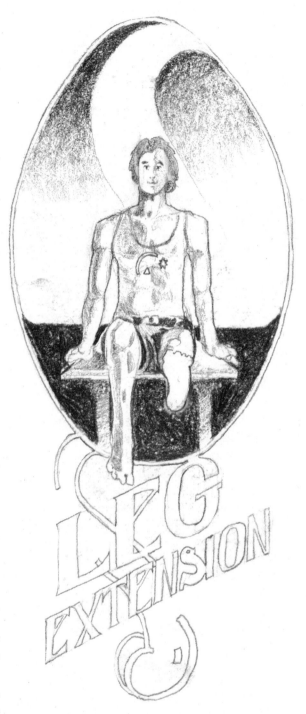

152

While it is quite *easy to load a pair of iron shoes to a hundred pounds,* it is not so easy to do anything with them . . .except pound dents in the floor.

From the stomach we move up to the chest (pectoralis majors), shoulders (deltoids) and arms (triceps). Almost anyone will benefit from work on these areas, but women who may be strong in other body parts will often show weakness in the chest and shoulders.

Fortunately, it is very easy to exercise the chest and shoulders. The best single routine for the chest, shoulders and arms is simple to learn, requires no equipment and because of the many possible variations can be anything from a cinch to a grueling bear to perform. I am speaking, of course, of the push-up.

A good number of people are completely unable to do a push-up. Others think they can, but can't because they are cheating. As runners we want to keep our muscles as long and limber as possible. Therefore we must attempt to get as much stretch as possible into our movements, which means no cheating.

The strict way to perform a push-up is to lie down in a prone position, palms against the ground at about shoulder level and slightly more than shoulder width apart. Keeping the body line flat (no bending at the waist or bottoms-up nonsense) press yourself away from the ground until your arms are perfectly straight. Your back should be flat, neither bowed or bent. Now lower yourself back to the prone position *until your chest touches the ground.* That's one. A complete push-up starts with the chest touching the ground and ends with the chest briefly touching the ground.

For people who want to stay loose, a better way of doing push-ups is to get a couple of handstand bars or thick books to rest your hands on. This way when you come down to the floor you get some real stretch across the chest.

Because your feet are lower than your hands, a regular push-up affects your lower pecs. I generally do the exercise in three stages and then repeat the cycle two to six times. First I do push-ups with feet on the ground; second elevated on a low box. Third, I get my feet at least three to four feet above the ground. The third position gives the upper pecs and deltoids a tremendous workout.

If you haven't done a push-up of any kind in years, or if you have never done a push-up in your entire life, you can slip right in via the wall-push-up.

Push your hand against a wall and walk back until you are three to four feet away…the further, the more difficult. Keeping your back flat, lower yourself toward the wall. Turn your head to the side at the last moment to avoid bashing your nose. Experiment with hand positioning to find the most comfortable position for yourself. An additional benefit of the wall push-up is you can use it as part of your calf-stretching routine.

As you get stronger, do more of these push-ups and move your feet further from the wall.

Another variation is the *bent-knee push-up.* This is begun the same way as the standard push-up, starting in the prone position. As you push up bend at the knee, keeping your lower legs in contact with the ground. Using the wall push-up and the bent-leg push-up for starters, soon you will be able to do a real push-up.

CHART ONE
Bent-Leg Push-Up (conditioning for standard push-up)

Rep/Set   Rest ten to thirty seconds between sets

Week	Sun.	Mon.	Tues.	Wed.	Thurs.	Fri.	Sat.
1.	1/2	1/3	2/3	2/4	3/3	3/4	3/4
2.	4/3	4/3	5/2	5/2	5/3	5/3	6/2
3.	6/2	6/3	6/3	7/2	7/2	8/2	8/2
4.	8/3	8/3	9/2	9/2	12/1	14/1	16/1

CHART TWO
Bent-Leg Push-Up (advanced conditioning for standard push-up)

Rep/Set   Rest ten to thirty seconds between sets

Week	Sun.	Mon.	Tues.	Wed.	Thurs.	Fri.	Sat.
1.	16/1	10/2	-0-	11/2	-0-	9/3	-0-
2.	9/3	10/3	-0-	10/3	-0-	11/3	-0-
3.	11/3	12/3	-0-	12/3	-0-	13/3	-0-
4.	15/2	16/2	-0-	18/2	-0-	20/2	-0-

CHART ONE
Beginning Standard Push-Up

Rep/Set   Begin in supine position, chest touching ground. Push-up with flat back until arms are straignt. Return to original position.

Week	Sun.	Mon.	Tues.	Wed.	Thurs.	Fri.	Sat.
1.	1/2	1/2	1/2	2/1	2/1	2/1	-0-
2.	2/2	-0-	2/	-0-	2/3	-0-	2/3
3.	-0-	3/2	-0-	3/2	-0-	3/3	-0-
4.	3/3	-0-	3/4	-0-	3/4	-0-	4/3
5.	-0-	4/3	-0-	4/4	-0-	4/4	-0-
6.	6/3	-0-	6/3	-0-	7/3	-0-	7/3
7.	-0-	8/2	-0-	8/2	-0-	10/1	-0-
8.	10/1	-0-	9/2	-0-	12/1	-0-	10/2

and so on . . .

Once you have gained confidence in your strength, vary the height of your feet in relation to your shoulder to exercise the lower, middle and upper parts of the chest and to give more work to your arms and shoulders.

Once you have built some upper-body strength with the push-ups you can go to another fine exercise that will do wonders for your back, shoulders, arms and, depending on how you do them, your chest as well. I speak of the *chin or pull-up*. Do I hear groans?

For some the pull-up is an absolute impossibility—at first. Get someone to help you. Find a bar that allows you to hang at full length, feet not touching the ground. You should have to give a little spring to grasp the bar. If you are unable to do a single chin, have someone grasp you around the waist and give you a *little lift* until your chin is over the bar. Controlling your descent, return to the hanging position. That's all for the first day. If you're new to this, don't attempt chins until after you've been doing push-ups for at least several weeks.

If you don't have anyone helping you, start with a lower bar and give a little spring to help get yourself up there. If you don't make it all the way up the first time, don't be concerned and don't try again until the next day.

The chin is a tough exercise and it's easy to do yourself in. If I come back after laying off a couple of months and whip out fifteen or so, the next day I can hardly lift my arms to brush my teeth.

CHART ONE
Beginning Chin-Up

Rep/Set   Either have someone help you by lifting slightly at your waist, or help yourself by springing lightly from the ground and pulling until your chin is above the bar. Let yourself down slowly and under control.

Week	Sun.	Mon.	Tues.	Wed.	Thurs.	Fri.	Sat.
1.	1/1	1/1	1/1	1/1	1/1	1/1	-0-
2.	1/2	1/2	1/2	1/2	1/2	1/2	-0-
3.	1/3	1/3	1/3	1/3	1/3	1/3	-0-
4.	2/1	2/1	2/1	2/1	2/1	2/1	-0-

By the time you complete the Chin-Up Chart One, you should be able to do at least one chin-up unaided and without jumping. As you work through the next chart do as many of the chins without help and without jumping as you can, then accept aid or spring up for the additional ones. Every few days attempt to do just one more without help.

CHART TWO
Beginning Chin-ups

Rep/Set   Do at least one chin-up without help and without jumping.

Week	Sun.	Mon.	Tues.	Wed.	Thurs.	Fri.	Sat.
1.	3/1	-0-	3/1	-0-	4/1	-0-	4/1
2.	-0-	2/2	-0-	2/2	-0-	3/2	-0-
3.	3/2	-0-	3/3	-0-	3/3	-0-	3/4
4.	-0-	3/4	-0-	4/3	-0-	4/3	-0-

The Perfect Marathon — Part II

If you have applied yourself to Chin-Up Charts One and Two, you should be able to do several chin-ups in strict style: full hanging position—pull up until chin is over the bar—return to full hanging position—hold for a large fraction of a second and pull up once more.

In the next chart, all chins should be performed in strict style.

CHART ONE
Chin-Ups Strict Style (Rep/Set)

Week	Sun.	Mon.	Tues.	Wed.	Thurs.	Fri.	Sat.
1.	2/1	-0-	2/1	-0-	3/1	-0-	3/1
2.	-0-	2/2	-0-	2/2	-0-	3/2	-0-
3.	3/2	-0-	4/1	-0-	4/1	-0-	3/2
4.	-0-	4/2	-0-	4/2	-0-	5/1	-0-
5.	4/2	-0-	5/2	-0-	5/2	-0-	5/2
6.	6/1	-0-	7/1	-0-	5/3	-0-	6/2
7.	-0-	6/2	-0-	5/3	-0-	5/4	-0-
8.	6/3	-0-	7/2	-0-	9/1	-0-	10/1

The next two exercises attack the deltoids and the complex of muscles across your back. They will, however, require a piece of equipment: the ubiquitous *chest expander*. It is sometimes seen as a flat strap of rubber with grips at each end and sometimes as a couple of handles with either springs or elastic cables attached. Somebody you know has a set lying around in a closet. Problem: unless you are a large person, six feet or better, most sets you find will be too long and too easy to use. You can make your own shorter pair by fitting a loop of surgical tubing to an existing pair of handles.

The spring-type expanders can be purchased at many department stores and sporting goods stores for about ten bucks—sometimes much less. The adjustable flat-band type can be purchased through Strength and Health Magazine. If you want the *"ne plus ultra"* and are willing to pay for it, look in Iron Man Magazine for the Samson Cable Set. The thing will work for someone as petite as Miki Gorman or as large as Mr. Universe. It's light and compact enough to stick in an overnight bag yet you can put enough resistance on it to stop a Clydesdale horse.

The first cable exercise is the lateral raise and attacks the deltoids almost exclusively. Stand straight, arms hanging, cables across the front of your legs. Your arms should be straight but the elbows not quite locked. Simultaneously raise both arms to the side, stretching the cable(s) across the front of your body. When your hands reach a point just above the shoulder level pause for a large fraction of a second and return to the starting position.

Begin this exercise with little resistance and only two reps. Over time work up to two sets of twenty, then add resistance and go back to one set of six. Work back up to two sets of twenty and start there, or start the process over again by adding more resistance.

The second exercise has three positions and is the primary cable movement. It's called the *Chest Expander*.

Cables in hand, hold your arms straight out in front of you, elbows unlocked and hands about neck level. Pull your hands back in a wide arc, bending your elbows slightly as you go. When you've stretched the cable as far as you can and your hands are as far back as they can go, you should look as if you're ready to fly. In fact, when this exercise is performed with dumbells, it is called *Dumbbell Flies*.

Perform the chest expander or cable flies from three starting postions: hands level with the neck, level with the nipples and just above the belly button. Begin with one set and one rep in each postion and work your way up the same as before.

There are many more good exercises you can do at home, the track or the gym with body weights, cables, barbells and machines, but when would you find time to run? Before we leave the stimulating subject of Supplementary Training, there is one more gadget that can really save your cookies: the stationary bicycle. Most gyms have them and home versions cost about fifty bucks and up. I hate the things and they are a bore to use, except when it's flooding outside or when a raging blizzard has gone on for a week. I've got one and I hardly ever use it. But when the weather turns rotten every runner for blocks around wants to borrow it. "Sorry friends, you'll just have to get in line."

Chapter VIII

Assuming that you have been training for over a year, have at least one successful marathon under your belt, and are a Type A Personality with a real need to win—that is to beat your own time, surpass your friends, and pick up some awards—how do you do it?

First, continue your long distance aerobic training. By now you will have discovered how many miles per week you can put in without injury. Don't do any more than that! Let's assume your maximum injury-free plateau is 80 miles per week. I suggest you cut back to 75% of that figure, or about 60 miles per week. If your maximum injury-free mileage is 60, cut back to 40 or 45 miles. This will be your maintenance level.

Continue at your maintenance level until approximately 9 weeks before your marathon. During this period include a program of endurance weight training, stretches, limbering and supplementary exercises such as bike riding.

Nine weeks from race day, add 5 miles to your weekly toll and continue to add 5 more miles every other week. During the 9th week incorporate some 10-second accelerations in your moderate length runs. "Accelerations?" Smoothly accelerate to a fast pace over a 10-second period then smoothly come down to an easy jog. Jog until your breathing is normal, then repeat for a total of 10. Do these 10 x 10 accelerations once or twice a week from the 9th through 6th weeks before a marathon.

During the 5th week drop the 10 x 10-*second* accelerations and substitute 10 x 220-*yard* accelerations. Accelerate to about 90% of maximum for 220 yards, then come down smoothly to a slow jog until breathing is normal or pulse is back to 120 beats per minute. After the first few 220 accelerations, you may want to walk/jog to normal. Do the 10 x 220s only once during the week, and the following week switch to 10 x 440 yards done in the same manner.

The third week before the marathon do the 10 x 440 accelerations on one day, and on another day run 5 miles for time. The second week before the marathon forget the accelerations, but do another 5-mile time trial...this is what you will use to calculate your marathon time from the Predictor Chart.

158

The week before the marathon is rest and maintenance time and a time to build your glycogen stores—see The Time Has Come: The Final Week.

If winning is really your desire, not only will you have to intensify your training over the last two months, but you will also probably have to get your weight down. For sure, you will have to be extra aware of pacing. As the overall time of your marathon drops, so does your margin for error. A four-hour marathoner can get by with a 15 or 20 second discrepancy in splits. A sub-three hour marathoner will be hurt by half that error.

Once you have actually used this system to train for a marathon, if you still feel that *more of something* is needed, add a 10K (6.2 mile) race every week beginning 8 or 9 weeks before the marathon. Discontinue these two weeks before the big one.

Chapter IX
Participating as A Spectator

Watching your first marathon is as exciting as running in the race. There are no *casual* observers.

Hundreds, even thousands of colorfully clad runners gather behind the starting line, their controlled frenzy infecting the crowd. People quiver with excitement clutching themselves, clutching each other—pressure building as the starter's gun rises in the air.

There is no distinction now between participant and observer. The entire mass of bodies is breathing in short, quick gasps like a single living entity. Everything is aquiver: runners, watchers, the ground itself.

The starter's finger tightens on the trigger—there's a massive intake of breath, then dead silence for a fraction of a second...and BANG!

A volcanic eruption: bodies rocket forward, people scream, onlookers rush alongside the runners unable to let go.

The outpouring of power, emotion and sound thunders unabated for ten minutes as the marathoners, practically out of control, surge past the one-mile mark into the distance.

The crowd relaxes and chatter begins, with frequent strange embarrassed pauses—vacant eyes—flushed cheeks. Everyone is coming down. Coming back to a sort of reality; ready to enjoy the race—to rest and then build to that final climax several hours away.

The marathon, like the "Circus of Dr. Lao," has something for everyone: the wand of Merlin or a visit from the Great God Pan. It can trigger an emotional and physical catharsis or provide a door to spiritual awakening. Most of all, the marathon is one heck of a lot of fun.

There is much to see in this *event of events,* and since the bulk of it lasts over four hours, you can see just about everything and still take a lunch break.

A must, of course, is the explosive start. For the first few seconds you can see an entire throng as a single rushing tidal wave. After that the marathon becomes a few torrents, a number of quick riverlets and a powerful slow-flowing Mississippi.

After the start try to find a bridge, a freeway overpass or a hill where you can see the line of the race. Try to do this early if it is to be an out-and-back course (13.1 miles in one direction and 13.1 miles back along the same route.)

Some of the faster runners will already be on the way back along the return route well before the bulk of the field even reaches the ten-or eleven-mile mark. These few front-runners are really in a race of their own.

Because the marathon is a people's event encompassing a wide variety of talents, needs and goals, it has an entirely different flavor than most other competitive sports where beating someone is the only thing. In the marathon there are many milestones, and everyone who finishes is a winner.

Beyond the first decision to train for and enter a marathon, every new long-distance runner faces a number of personal goals that have little or nothing to do with other people in the race. Primary is to finish...preferably running; if necessary, walking, crawling or dragging yourself along by your fingernails. Sometimes, due to pain and injury, it is necessary even for experienced marathoners to drop out. It is difficult to convey the feelings one has when such an event takes place. The only cure is to go out and run another one...and finish.

After discovering that (s)he can actually run a marathon and finish as a whole human being, not a hollow shell, the next goal usually chosen is to break four hours (4:00:00). This requires an average pace of slightly more than nine minutes per mile (09:09.24). Generally, when trying to break four hours, a runner will use a flat nine-minute pace which gives a four-minute cushion. Besides, nine minutes and no seconds is an easy figure for an oxygen-starved brain to cope with.

People will often have personal, intermediate goals, but the next big one is to break three and a half hours (3:30:00), an eight-minute (+) pace. This is a rather neat jump from the previous four hours, but it has other things to recommend it besides neatness.

If you are a woman, a 3:20:00 in any certified marathon will qualify you to run in Boston. A male over 40 requires a 3:10 to qualify. That's right folks, not just any old duffer can run in the great Boston Marathon; unless the duffer happens to belong to the American Medical Jogging Association; or maybe another special interest group or two; or is willing to run without a number.

Between 3:30:00 and three hours flat every minute is hard won, but the real obstacle is that last second that will bring a runner to 2:59:59. Any male under forty who wishes to run Boston officially and with honor, now must have run a certified marathon during the previous year in a time of 2:50 or better.

Of the thousands of runners entering marathons annually, less than 24% will break three hours...and most of these not by much. About an equal number will drop out before the race is over. Most of the action is between three hours and three-thirty, then it slacks off and picks up again at four hours, so you have plenty of time to move around and seek the prime vantage points.

The marathon is a group and family affair, so many people pack picnic lunches and settle down where the view is good. If you come alone, you can probably find a group to join; these are very friendly folk.

The Perfect Marathon — Part II

In your search for the perfect site, consider a long curve which can provide a dramatic sweep, or the crest of a hill. If you'd like to make yourself beloved of all the runners, pack an ice chest with a bottle of cold water and lay in a supply of paper cups—the kind with accordion sides. As the runners come over the crest and onto the flat, hand out the cups of water. Late in the race don't expect a response other than dumb acceptance, but deep down inside they'll love you for what you're doing.

Don't hand out plastic cups which will shatter in uncoordinated hands. The marathoner can crush the tops of paper cups without breaking them and carry the water along.

Many kind and well-meaning nurturers hand out orange slices, fruit juices and even pieces of hard candy. What a distance runner needs the most, especially during hot weather, is cold water, lots of it, and maybe some ice beginning at the twelve- or fifteen-mile mark.

All marathons have official watering stops, but these frequently run out of water and run out of ice even sooner. In my opinion, the more unofficial cold water stations the better.

If you are really into cold orange slices, please pass them out at the end of the race—along with Coke and beer—we'll definitely need them then.

So you'll feel more a part of the event, treat yourself to an official T-shirt. All runners get one and you can help cover some of the expenses of a race by getting one for yourself. They're usually available at the race site where the runners register.

While you're at the registration site, how about volunteering for some official function. Races are chronically short of timers. Their job is to station themselves at one of the mile markers and call out elapsed time to the passing runners. This is an extremely important function, and essential for the runners who are attempting to establish an even pace.

In addition to calling out times at the mile markers, other timers are stationed at the 5, 10, 15, 20 and 25-mile splits to record every runner's times for the official race records.

Watering stops often need volunteers, especially to give the regular people an occasional break—but don't give up on the idea of establishing your own unofficial stop.

If you are free to get away, about two hours after the start of the race get back to the finish line. Depending on who's running, the first finisher can come across in anything between 2:09 and 2:45—a race official will give you a good estimate. The next runner may cross anywhere from a few seconds to ten minutes later . . . maybe even later than that.

The crowd is excited when the first few runners cross, but nothing like you'd expect. The media interview the winner, almost always missing the best show.

Minute by minute the spectator enthusiasm grows, until by three hours it is wild. When the first woman crosses everyone goes bananas. From then on it is an absolute madhouse: yelling, screaming, cheering, weeping, laughing and crying all at the same time.

For the runner the first huge thrill—and it's mind-bending—occurs at the start and lasts for the first mile. From then on it's low-level ecstacy for ten to twelve miles. If a runner is well-trained and pacing, he or she will run much of the mileage, between twelve and twenty-five, in and out of a shallow hypnotic state. At twenty-five miles the pressure goes on and as twenty-six approaches the skin begins to prickle and chills go up and down the spine.

For the last couple of minutes runners experience a raging high, finishing in a blazing climax as they burn through the finish chute and become immortal. *The spectator experiences this ecstacy almost continuously for a solid hour.*

Don't leave. Mingle with the recovering runners. Get them cold things to drink. Help them get up, get down—help them walk. Listen to their stories, their visions, their what-happened and what-might-have-happened. Listen to the lies (dreams), the plans—what they're going to do next time, you-just-wait-and-see.

Mingle long enough and listen close enough and you may just find yourself, a few days later, struggling to complete that first agonizing but oh-so-sweet mile.

Chapter X

On race day it is the marathoner who is hero. A month later everyone loves the photographer.

Along with baby's first step or a kid's first haircut, few things lend themselves so well to pictures as a first (second, third or tenth) marathon. Weeks, months, even years later, photographs and movies help rekindle much of the excitement, tension, joy and nostalgia of that marvelous *event of events*.

The photographic possibilities actually begin months before the race—perhaps with the first step of the first quarter-mile.

As the months go by photographs will record the gradual changing of an ordinary human being into a being glowing with inner fire. There will be records of the low points, when it was sheer hell just to think about putting on a pair of jogging shoes, and high points, when running forever would have been paradise.

Milestones are great photographic subjects: purchase of the first pair of jogging shoes, first fancy shorts or training outfit. Some people like to record the first blister or case of black toe, but I'd just as soon forget about those.

Throughout the training period there will probably be a number of short races from one to six miles. Take pictures. It's a good way to get practice in shooting under unpredictable conditions.

Photographing a footrace isn't the easiest thing in the world. Your subjects are always moving, changing position and getting in the way of one another. The backgrounds change from simple to fantastically complicated and your light changes from white-bright to shadow-black.

You can be so rushed trying to get a shot off that you move the camera and blur the image. If you happen to hold the camera steady there is still a good chance that the swiftly moving figures will blur themselves.

So you get lucky and don't move the camera, your shutter speed is fast enough to capture the speeding figures—still the picture doesn't come out. The background is sharp and the people are out-of-focus.

Better to practice your photographic technique during preliminary races long before the big one arrives. By the time marathon day rolls around you want to be as comfortable with the situation as possible.

Getting the good ones during athletic events is so difficult that experienced pros come up with a high percentage of out-of-focus, blurred and miscomposed images. They partially cover themselves by taking at least ten times as many pictures as they can possibly use. In addition, there are secrets that will help you come up with some unforgettable treasures.

If you already have a camera(s) it will probably do. If you'd like to buy something specifically for recording *race history*, but don't want to get in too deep, I recommend a compact range finder camera such as the Olympus RC (35mm) and a powerful portable flashgun such as the Vivitar 283. I've used both these items for years and can't recommend them too highly.

The Olympus RC has a number of features that make it attractive for sports photography. I'll mention two: it has a semi-wide-angle lens with good depth of field, and it will synchronize with a flashgun at any speed up to one five-hundredth of a second. Why this is important, I'll cover shortly.

If you own a 35mm SLR with interchangeable lenses, the following additional lenses (in order of importance) would be helpful.

For many years I've used a wide-angle lens on my Nikon (Vivitar 28mm f/2.5) to photograph in tight situations and to add dramatic perspective to otherwise rather ordinary shots. The 28mm wide-angle is particularly effective shooting the mass of runners head-on just as the gun goes off. Because of its depth characteristics, it's almost impossible to get an out-of-focus shot. Lately I have also been using a Vivitar 17mm f/3.5 (not a fish-eye) to get some spectacular shots.

One trick I do with the 17mm is to prefocus at about a foot and a half and stick the camera blindly out into the course. Just when a runner is about to slam into the lens I squeeze off a shot and pull the camera out of the way. The entire figure shows up in the picture, sharp, clear and dramatic.

For your first extra lens I recommend a wide-angle. The most useful one is a 28mm and after that (if you really take a lot of pictures) an 18mm or 17mm non-fish-eye. Don't waste your money on a 35mm—too mild, and I don't think they are very versatile. Ten years ago, yes...today, no.

Second on the list of extra lenses is either a 135mm telephoto or zoom (something on the order of 70mm—210mm would be good). 135mm allows you to get some nice close-ups of runners when you can't move in close. The advantage of the zoom is that you can keep the figure the same size in the viewfinder as (s)he runs toward you and away, and 210mm gives you much more magnification when you need it. With the 135mm lens, if the runner gets so close that the head and feet are cut off, you are pretty much out of luck—unless you can run backwards faster than the marathoner can run forward. With the 70mm—210mm you can zoom out to 70mm, cutting the size of the figure almost in half compared to the 135mm lens.

The 135mm is a great lens, no doubt about that, but the zoom costing two or three times as much does have an important edge in sports photography.

Here's a final lens that can give some great shots, but it is a seldom-used luxury and not that much fun to lug around. I am, of course, speaking of a long telephoto. The one I use is a 400mm. If you are more familiar with binocular terminology than with camera lenses, 400mm is about eight power.

At any given marathon I might take ten or fifteen long telephoto shots from bridges, freeway overpasses and nearby hills. It is practically useless for close-ups of fast-moving objects due to its nil depth of field. Actually I didn't get mine for photographing marathons, I got it for taking pictures of lions where getting close was not a consideration.

Should you decide to get a 400 (they are fun) and price is a factor, the best deal going is the Spiratone 400mm f/6.3 Plura-coat Preset Tele. It was originally recommended to me by Modern Photography magazine, and I haven't regretted the purchase.

Armed with a diverse range of equipment, there are still common approaches to getting clean, sharp, well-exposed pictures.

The Perfect Marathon — Part II

Unless you're filming in the snow or at the beach, use the most sensitive film you can get your hands on: 400 or 500 ASA. A sensitive film will enable you to use a small f/stop (small -f/16, f/11, f/8, f/5.6, f/4, f/3.5, f/2, f/1.4-large) which gives you greater depth of field (area in focus) and a high shutter speed which will stop action.

Ideally you should try to use a shutter speed of 1/250th of a second or faster. If you can use an even faster speed you will greatly improve the sharpness (not focus) of the runners.

One of the reasons I suggested practice on less important races is to cut out the fiddling around. If you have to fiddle with your camera while a runner is coming toward you, (s)he is either going to be out-of-focus or out-of-the-country by the time you snap the shutter. Even cutting the fiddling, chances are the image will still be a little fuzzy. Here's why I suggest a sensitive film.

Let's say you're using a not-very-sensitive film (ASA 25), your camera is set at f/4 and is focused at 10 feet. Your margin of error will be only about two feet. Not much chance of keeping a runner in focus. Suppose everything's the same but you're using ASA 400 film. With that film in the camera your lens would be set at f/16 instead of f/4. At f/16 and the camera focused to ten feet again, your margin for error is now about fifteen feet...nice, huh!

These figures are for a 50mm lens. The tele lenses give you less margin, but the 17mm wide-angle at f/16 would have everything sharp from your own feet out to the planet Mars.

If you're new to photography the figures may be confusing; just remember that bright light and/or sensitive film will help keep things in focus and stop motion.

Here's another trick: prefocus. Pick an interesting area along the route, focus on it carefully and wait. When a runner pounds into the x-marks-the-spot, squeeze off a good one. Even better, have someone walk toward you until they almost completely fill the viewfinder. Have them stop and very carefully focus. Now look at the lens barrel, check the distance setting and remember it. All you have to do in the future (with that particular lens) is prefocus, point, and when the runner comes to you, fire off a shot.

Now that we've solved all the shaking, zipping by and focusing problems, we come to exposure. This is difficult, especially if you're a beginner or are using an automatic exposure camera.

Automatic cameras are really wonderful for snapshots under fairly mundane conditions. They even have adjustments for some slightly *strange* conditions. However, their little pea-brains become confused when the *strange* conditions change from shot to shot and you just don't have time to explain things to them (through their little controls).

Let's say you don't have an automatic camera, but a manual one with a fine built-in light meter or even a first class hand-held meter. Will things be better—easier? Yes, a little. But not much.

Taking light reading is tricky. Tricky but fun if you let it be. Let's say you're trying to take a picture of a runner about fifteen feet from your position. Let's also assume that you took a light reading off the previous runner and set the camera so you'd be *ready*. Perfect exposure? Maybe; maybe not.

Let's suppose the runner is brightly lit, but the background (twenty-five feet away) is a dense thicket of dark trees and brush. What happens? Your meter, in camera or out, will read the scene in its entirety and decide that you need to let in enough light to properly expose the trees. This will almost always cause your figure to be overexposed. Depending on the type of meter, averaging or center-weighted, the runner will either be slightly overexposed or completely burnt out.

What would happen if you tried to take a picture of a runner cresting a hill backed up by a brilliant cloudless sky? The opposite of the first situation, naturally. The meter or automatic exposure camera wants to bring the sky down correctly so the figure will probably wind up as a near dead-black silhouette.

There are lots of fancy computations and even a very special (and very expensive) meter to solve these problems, but I have a nice home-type method that works every time and costs nothing...is that cheap enough?

Just stick out your hand so it is lit about the same as your subject will be and take a reading. You could also use what is called an 18% gray card, or even just stick the camera in a friend's face. Using the hand, face, or card method, the reflecting surface so dominates the field of view that backgrounds have little or no effect on light readings. You just have to be careful that your hand and the potential subject receive similar light.

From all this you will have probably surmised that if you take tight shots of your runners you will have fewer lighting problems—and you are correct...which brings us to my next handy hint. Don't hang back. The closer you get to the subject the more detail. Sure, sometimes you'll want a long shot to establish a feeling of the overall event, or a two or three shot to build tension...but that's only sometimes.

The shots you're going to treasure are the ones of a single figure filling the frame: every feature sharp, every straining muscle delineated, every drop of sweat reflecting a pinpoint of light.

If you use a small f/stop, a high shutter speed, frame your figure tightly, prefocus and hold the camera as steady as a rock, you'll get images so super-lifelike they'll jump right out of the picture.

Now that you've read, learned, practiced and perfected these rules, let's break one. It'll be fun.

The race is progressing across your field of view, at right angles to your position. The background is either uninteresting or terribly jumbled and confusing...in any case it can add little or nothing to your picture—or can it? Frame your subject and hold the runner in the viewfinder by panning smoothly *with* the action. Squeeze off the shot. If you do it right and if you have a bit of luck your picture will be a wow...artistically streaked background and runners sharp and clear.

A little time and practice and the technique will become second nature—which is good. Technique should never come between you and the picture, or between you and a good time. There is a way to practically eliminate technique as it relates to figuring exposure, shutter speed and camera steadiness.

Several pages back I suggested that if you are a casual photographer who wants to buy a camera especially to photograph the marathon, you should consider a combination of the Olympus RC and the Vivitar 283 flashgun. Here's why. The only way to be completely sure of your light is to bring your own. In practical terms that means a flashgun. Most cameras will take pictures only with an electronic flashgun when they are set at a relatively slow shutter speed: 1/30th—1/25th of a second.

On a bright day the slow shutter speed allows an exposure by ambient light and another exposure by flash. On a single frame of film you will have two pictures, one sharp, one blurred.

With an Olympus RC you can take electronic flash pictures at 1/500th of a second. At 1/500th of a second shutter speed and a lens setting of f/16, ambient light rarely becomes a factor to consider; your subject is effectively without light. The Vivitar is a powerful automatic flash. It will give you the proper exposure. Not only that, but it will really freeze action due to a flash duration of 1/1000th—1/30,000th of a second depending on subject distance.

In order to get this combination to work you have to do only four things: stick ASA 200 film in the camera; set the camera at f/16 and 1/500th of a second; put the flash on automatic. From then on, no matter how fast the action or how poor the light, all you have to do is focus on the runners and everything should be sharp, clear and well-exposed.

It's one thing to know *how* to take good pictures and quite another to decide *what* to take. Everyone has ideas on what's important to cover during the marathon experience, and weeks later almost everyone is sorry they didn't take more—that is except Linda Lindsey, official photographer and den mother of the West University Pacers King Kong Running Team. Linda is a past master who has taken hundreds of color photographs before, during and after every race. Because she uses color *negative* film we get color prints back from the lab and I can also make black and white enlargements.

Using Linda's photographic coverage as a guide, a few of my ideas and those of other friends, here are some suggestions—what you can record for posterity (or next month's postmortem):

The night-before gathering around the ritual spaghetti dinner or six-pack of beer. The pre-dawn awakening (sans alarm clock) and the breaking of the fast with juice, coffee and banana—or whatever.

The Perfect Marathon — Part II

Be sure to get pictures of the early morning stumbling around, the suiting up and the stuffing of everyone into the car to get to the race site. You'll want to remember standing in line to get the race packet and, for sure, get pictures of chest numbers being pinned on. Greasing-up is always good for a few dirty laughs, so are the shots of hundreds of nervous people standing in line at the portable outhouses.

Even though it's obvious, don't miss the shots of runners and spectators milling about the starting line.

You will, of course, get the start of the race itself. And come hell or high water, don't miss the finish!

In my last race, the best one to date, I zipped in about ten minutes sooner than expected. No one had a camera ready. I got lots of congratulations and there were plenty of pictures of other parts of the marathon, but it was a disappointment not to have a finish picture of myself—beard covered with ice and steam pouring from my nostrils.

Linda said it was my fault for coming in like a show-off. Jim had nothing to say. He was too down-in-the-dumps, having been forced out of the race with terrible back pains.

After the marathon you'll want pictures of the dehydrated runners sucking up gallons of beer, Coke and anything else wet they can get their hands on. There'll be pictures of tired but happy friends greeting each other and falling down in each others' arms. There will be shots of runners comparing blisters and collapsed around the hotel room in utter exhaustion. And finally,there will be someone checking the calendar, looking for the date of the next marathon.

Chapter XI

My friend Jerry Miller says the only *real* secret of a successful marathon is pimento cheese sandwiches. Just goes to show I'm not the only one with funny ideas.

Funny or not, if certain things work, THEY WORK! The scientific approach is certainly a valuable one, but it's no place to stop—the mind must be considered! If a ritual works for you, even if it has no scientific value as measured in a lab, its value on the course is "proof" enough.

Personally I think the greatest trick of all is the weekly long run and I believe the value is as much psychological as physiological. Other runners feel that the weekly totals are the most important, even if they contain no really long runs.

By questioning large numbers of marathon finishers and comparing their answers to finish times (and improvement of finish times), certain procedures and experiences were found to have an across-the-board importance. Here they are, all of them important but not necessarily in order of importance.

Twenty-Mile Runs As twenty-mile weekly runs accumulate, marathon times tend to get better. First-time marathoners with slow and difficult finishes typically have run no twenty-milers or at most one, and this during the week prior to the race.

Weekly Totals Over Sixty Miles The more weeks (not including marathon week or the week prior) of sixty miles and more, the better the time. Slow finishers tend to have had only one or two long weeks and these just prior to the race when they should have been resting.

Low Body Weight/Low Percentage of Body Fat As the percentage of body fat goes down, speeds and ease of running goes up. I heard some doctor once say that taking off ten pounds of useless weight does more good than adding ten miles to the weekly total. Another figures that—within reason—every two pounds of unneeded weight that is lost results in a one percent increase in running efficiency.

Experience Times tend to get better after one has run the first marathon. This is in part due to the actual experience. Equally important is the fact that one will have accumulated more total training mileage and more long runs after taking part in several marathons.

The Perfect Marathon — Part II

Pace Well-trained runners who fail to finish or who finish in a much poorer time than expected typically went out for the first ten miles at a much faster pace than an average of the finish time would have required. Energy burned at too fast a rate during the first half of the marathon cannot be recovered during the second half.

O.K., that was the result of surveys, broad questioning and computer printouts. It applies to all of us more or less equally. What follows is a potpourri of tricks, hints, secrets, ideas and suggestions I've gathered over the years from runners of every caliber: those reaching for a four-hour marathon and those reaching for an Olympic Gold Medal. I've even included a few of my personal insanities.

These inclusions are in no particular order, some are contradictory and some may seem to make no sense at all…but; every one of these ideas has something in common. They have worked for the people who suggested them. Maybe it's mental. Maybe it's physical. It may even be metaphysical—who cares—the ideas work for someone.

I make no recommendations. Like P.T. Barnum I present the following for your elucidation, education and entertainment.

Take Off Your Socks I know one runner who trains with heavy sweat socks and races sockless. When he tried racing one time with the sweat socks on, it added ten minutes to his marathon finish time and his feet felt heavy during the entire race. Ah, the mind of man.

Run Lots of Steep Hills Running hills builds strong legs, intestinal fortitude and general stick-to-itness. Hill work is an essential part of any marathon training program.

Don't Bother Running Hills Unless you plan on running in a hilly marathon, hills are a complete waste of time and build muscles totally useless for running long distance.

Run on the Outside This is a fine trick that I credit to Ralph Nolte—and it works. When you are running at the track, especially if you are training with a friend or two, always run in an outside lane. Not only will you be running slightly more than a quarter-mile each lap, but you will also be required to run slightly faster on the curves than your companions. The differences will be hardly noticeable at the time. However, they do add up.

Running Ramps Here's another training secret that Ralph just let out of the bag. He starts using it about two months before a marathon. Generally there are bleachers next to an outdoor quarter-mile track and often there are a pair of access ramps behind the stands. Ralph jogs a couple of miles to warm up, then for an additional two miles he will veer off every quarter of a mile and include the up and down ramps in the circuit. This provides one heck of a workout, especially if you charge up the ramp, then glide down the other side. After the initial few weeks he begins upping the mileage until he is doing as much as ten miles with forty trips up and down the ramps. If you decide to do this, I'd advise you not to try eight trips up and down at first. Start with one trip and do the routine only a couple of times a week.

Week	Sun.	Mon.	Tues.	Wed.	Thurs.	Fri.	Sat.
1.	0	0	1	0	0	1	0
2.	0	0	2	0	0	2	0
3.	0	0	4	0	0	4	0
4.	0	0	6	0	0	6	0
5.	0	0	8	0	0	8	0

If there aren't any ramps you could run the bleachers, but they are not nearly as much fun and there's a certain danger involved.

Improve the View On some days I just don't feel like running. A sure cure, for me at least, is to find someone physically attractive and run behind them. It's amazing how time will fly. I remember once I was running at the track with some friends and our spirit just wasn't in it. We were poking along at about a ten-minute pace ready to call it quits when this fantastic-looking female whizzed by us. Without thinking we found ourselves clipping along at a 7:30 pace and it was five miles before we realized that we had quit complaining. What brought us out of our reverie was the girl glancing back and asking us if it was OK for her to follow and look for awhile. We obliged.

Don't Run In A New T-Shirt Be sure to wash a new T-shirt or tank top several times before you wear it to run in. This is especially true of the shirts you receive for entering marathons and other races. The material and the design tend to be quite rough at first and will abrade your skin, particularly under the arms, at the shoulders and neck and on the nipples. Even when you do the marathon in a very soft t-shirt or tank top, these rub areas should have an ample coating of Vaseline. Put a coating of Vaseline on the inside of your thighs before you start the marathon or any long run.

Grease Your Feet See above.

Stay Away From Boats Edmund Strickler, formerly chubby dentist and now a "lean and mean" marathoner, has this advice: don't mess with boats during training season. Ed smacked the end of his toe while standing in the water trying to maneuver his yachtlet and wound up having to go under famed Sport Podiatrist Bill Van Pelt's knife for surgery. After a couple of weeks the pain began to go away, but the toe was still a little floppy. I suppose I should be more sympathetic with Dr. Strickler's painful mishap, but the way I figure it, maybe now I'll have half a chance of beating Ed in a marathon.

Don't Wear The Same Socks Twice Be sure to wash your socks, shorts and shirts before you wear them a second time...you will keep your friends and keep your skin. Dry salt is rough on the body and stiff salty socks will rub blisters.

Drying Out After a run, hang your stuff to dry before you throw them in the hamper or stuff them in a closet. Your shoes and running garb will last longer and your family will be much easier to get along with. You might also consider spraying your shoes with Dr. Scholl's Shoe Deodorizer, which will also tend to keep your family happier.

Some runners, especially those who train without socks, periodically wash their shoes. If you do so, dry them in a cold dryer or in front of a fan. Don't use heat, or the soles may fall off.

Keep Moving Don't sit down right after a run. Keep on jogging or at least walking for a quarter of a mile or so. This will extend the conditioning period, enhance circulation, help prevent injuries and speed recovery after heavy training. Under certain conditions sitting down right after strenuous exercise can cause everything from uncomfortable cramps to death.

There have been cases of people doing hard workouts in the cold and sitting down immediately afterwards in a heated car—never to get up again. Contrary to popular belief the heart is *not the only pump* in the circulatory system. The action of the muscles provides a tremendous assist to the return flow. If you sit down instead of warming-down and cooling-down you will be seriously impeding circulation and putting a severe and unnecessary burden on the heart. I want to make it very clear to any reporters, reviewers and runners who may be reading this: this is a warning against sitting, not against running.

Break Them In When you buy a new pair of jogging shoes, wear them around the house for a week before you begin to use them in light training, then wait another couple of weeks before you use them for any long mileage.

Stay On The Level After your shoes have been broken in there will probably be some slight wear indications on the sole. Fill these areas in with soft plastic from a hot-melt glue-gun. Do this before the heels become worn over and you'll avoid a good number of foot and leg problems. Your shoes will hold up longer as well.

Be Prepared Carry toilet paper with you on long runs and during the marathon. If the need strikes, and it sometimes does for a significant minority of runners, take full advantage of woods, portapots, gas stations and private homes.

Always Run With People Better Than Yourself This will make you try harder and make it more difficult to goof-off.

Always Train With People Worse Than Yourself This will build your ego and give you someone to lord it over.

The Perfect Marathon — Part II

Take It Easy On Yourself If you aren't enjoying your run, quit and come back another day when you are in better spirits. After all, running isn't the most important thing in the world, so why should you do it if it isn't fun!

Stick With It No Matter What If it starts to drizzle, or if your friends aren't there, or if you just aren't enjoying yourself, don't give up. You came to run and run you will until you have completed a certain minimum you've set for yourself. Things that are worthwhile don't always come easy, so don't quit unless stopped by pain, injury or dangerous conditions.

Something For Nothing (3+3=6½) Split your medium runs into two sessions. During hot weather two three-mile runs, early morning and late evening, will probably be easier than one six- mile jog. Two runs require twice the number of stretching sessions, warm-ups, warm-downs and cool-offs, significantly lengthening the conditioning period. You feel as if you are taking it easy, but you're actually getting more benefit.

Cool Feet At the end of your post-workout shower, run straight cold water on your feet, ankles and tendons. This will help prevent and/or soothe minor aches and soreness. Works even better with a Shower Massage.

Have A Ball Press down on a small hard ball with your bare foot and roll it around. Feels good on sore tired tootsies. See above.

A Little Extra Ride your bike to the track instead of taking your car.

Easy Carbohydrate Loading After your long run of fifteen or twenty miles, treat yourself to ice cream, or better yet, cold apple juice. The long run will deplete a good deal of glycogen from your leg muscles. If you drink apple juice, say half a gallon, during the couple of hours right after a long run, much of it will be converted to muscle fuel and stored in the leg muscles. Give yourself a day's rest and on the third day you should be brimming with energy and ready to begin your training week.

Making Time Fly I know poeple who do complicated math while they jog, others who do word games. Cheryl Robbi-Du (member of the King Kong running team, Fay Wray division) sings songs to herself. What songs I don't know, but probably Vivaldi for the sprints and Wagner for the long haul. I disconnect my brain and go off somewhere else and let my body do the running, returning every half-mile or so to check things out. It's often quite a surprise to return and find myself in unfamiliar surroundings, not having a clue to how I got there.

Sometimes when I'm disconnected I visit interesting places and strange worlds. Other times I may become hyperaware of my surroundings both animate and inanimate, disconnecting only from the actual supervision of running.

I've seen a few people jogging with portable radios in their hands or radio earphones on. Somehow these seem unhealthy to me, but to each his own.

It's All A Big Joke During long training runs and during the first half of a marathon I pass time by joking and talking with fellow runners. Usually by twelve or fifteen miles it's getting difficult to get people to grunt, let alone laugh. After fifteen miles the line of the race is so spread out there generally isn't anyone to talk to—except for calling out encouragement to the walkers and receiving it from bystanders.

Do It In The Dark There seems to be some agreement that time and miles go by faster in the dark. Many runners report *altered states of consciousness* occuring much more frequently in the dark, especially when running alone—others report muggings.

Mix Work And Play A group of professors at the University of Texas in Austin schedule a daily one-hour noon-till-one o'clock run and lecture instead of lunch. Each day a different member of the small group is scheduled to present the lecture.

Hills In The Flatlands If you really feel you need hill work and there aren't any hills around, find an exceptionally tall parking garage and run the ramps either early in the morning or late at night when there aren't any cars around. The garage should be tall enough so it takes you about three minutes or longer to reach the top.

Hilly Marathons If you plan to run in the Boston Marathon, or any other marathon with hills, you will need to train on hills. Start about two months before the race and work up very slowly so you don't damage yourself or exhaust yourself.

Mile-High Marathons If you plan to run in a high-altitude marathon, train at least a month at the same altitude or higher. If you don't, the marathon will be no fun, you will do poorly and you probably will feel sick.

Smog If you run early in the day the smog may be less severe. If the day is really bad, train on an indoor track or forgo running and use a stationary bike.

More For The Legs Do dozens, if not hundreds of partial squats (knee bends) in addition to running. This will really work those muscles without pounding the joints. The squats may be performed either with or without additional weight.

Writ In Stone Make up a rigid daily, weekly and monthly training schedule and stick with it no matter what.

Laissez-faire Decide on a reasonable minimum daily mileage. On days when you don't have a lot of spirit or energy, run just the minimum. When you feel fine, full of energy and the weather is good, run longer and train harder.

Carry A Stopwatch Always carry a stopwatch when you train. It will help you gauge your improvement and keep you from getting lazy.

Don't Carry A Stopwatch Constantly using a stopwatch makes training too mechanical, puts on too much pressure and leads to injury. Only use a stopwatch for special occasions: for time trials, to measure the overall time of a long run and during the marathon.

Final Tip Jim Lindsey says, you should always keep a few secrets to yourself.

Glossary

Accelerations Consecutive, eight to fifteen second speed runs alternated with recovery jogs of 52 to 45 seconds. Accelerations train the "fast twitch" muscles without causing oxygen debt. This is considered by some to be an ideal method for increasing oxygen uptake among distance runners. Ten to twenty consecutive accelerations are ample. See **Intervals**.

Aerobic Exercise Exercise performed at a level at which the body can take in and utilize all the oxygen it needs for a given task. At this level work can be performed almost indefinitely. Research indicates that aerobic exercise at a pulse rate between 120 and 150 beats per minute, performed for a minimum of 30 minutes three times a week, will enhance cardiovascular/pulmonary function. Marathon running and training, except for brief periods, should be run aerobically. See **Conversational Pace**.

Anaerobic Exercise Exercise at a level where oxygen debt is incurred, resulting in heavy breathing, a constant and progressive lowering of efficiency and eventual forced cessation of activity. During marathon training no more than 5% of the running program should be at an anaerobic level. See **Conversational Pace**.

Banana Breakfast the morning of your marathon. High in potassium, an electrolyte lost in perspiration.

Boston Qualifying As of this writing, unless you are a member of an exempt group such as the American Medical Jogging Association you must have achieved the following times or better in a certified marathon during the previous 12 months in order to officially enter the Boston Marathon; Women 3:20:00, Masters Men (40 years of age or older) 3:10:00, Open 2:50:00.

Breathing Something done through the mouth and nose. The idea is to get in as much air as possible.

Burn Out A feeling of depression following a too long period of heavy training. Often occurs a month or six weeks before an important race. See **Peaking**.

Carbohydrate Depletion Short term elimination of most carbohydrates from the diet in preparation for Carbohydrate Loading. Carbohydrates are found mainly in baked goods, grains, legumes, starchy vegetables and items containing added sugar and other nutritional (sic) sweeteners. See **Carbohydrate Loading**.

Carbohydrate Loading Also called Packing. A short term diet in which fats and proteins are de-emphasized and *complex* carbohydrates are stressed. The purpose is to saturate the muscles with glycogen during the few days prior to a marathon. Muscles run on glycogen, and the more glycogen available in the working muscles the greater the inefficiency during a distance run and the quicker the recovery time. Carbohydrate Loading is more effective if preceded by a depletion phase, however neither regimen should be undertaken without a doctor's approval. See **Carbohydrate Depletion**.

Cardiac Patients Get your doctor's permission before you do any exercise. While a number of former heart attack victims have trained for and successfully completed marathons (in particular the difficult Hawaii Marathon) this sport is not for everyone. A far greater number of former cardiac patients have gone on to make jogging and long distance non-competitive running an integral part of their new and healthier life style, but again this is not for everyone. Get an OK before you go on.

Change Frequently causes injuries. Abrupt change in training surfaces, shoes, speed, length of individual runs, length of weekly totals will eventually cause some kind of breakdown. The key to success is consistency and adaptation . . . allow enough time to adapt to new situations. See **Injuries**.

Chronometer A highly accurate timepiece that should have a stopwatch function; most useful if worn on the wrist. Digital readouts are the easiest to use, and the plastic ones seem to resist perspiration the best. They weigh only about half an ounce complete with battery. See **Stop Watch**.

Conversational Pace The fastest pace at which you can run/jog and still carry on a reasonably comfortable conversation. If you are forced to gasp for breath when you try to talk, you are racing not training. See **Aerobic Exercise**.

Cool Off A period of minimal exercise or walking just prior to final stretching and limbering movements. See **Warm Up** and **Warm Down**.

Cramps Something that can occur anytime during a marathon and often just after. If it's in the calf or hamstring, carefully stretch the muscle to its greatest length and massage deeply and towards the heart. If the cramp is in the diaphram, slow down a bit or walk if necessary. Breathe quick and shallow from the stomach or deep and slow, hold your hands over your head, pinch your upper lip until the diaphram cramp goes away . . .something is bound to work. Long term cure for cramps is stretching, limbering, strength building through progressive resistance training, and eating food rich in calcium and potassium.

Danger What comes from 1) Cars, 2) Creeps, 3) Dogs. 1) Watch where you're going and wear bright reflective clothing. 2) Don't run alone and in dark or isolated areas—carry a whistle and perhaps a can of mace. 3) Carry a wooden switch or radio aerial for a show of power.

D.C.M. Doctor of Chiropractic Medicine. The medical professional of choice for many distance runners especially when the problem seems to be mechanical. While some runners and other athletes practically worship chiropractors, others wouldn't go to one on a bet. If you do opt for a D.C.M., try to find one who has had extensive experience with runners. See **D.P.M.** and **M.D.**

Discomfort Something to be expected from time to time during training and racing. Often occurs before the body is fully warmed up and disappears during an extended run. May also be caused by an overly full or active alimentary canal—empty it; improperly fitting shoes—change shoes; or body parts rubbing—use Vaseline, lose weight. See **Pain** and **Vaseline**.

D.P.M. Doctor of Podiatric Medicine/Foot Doctor. If you think you may need one, check to see if he or she is a member of the American Academy of Podiatric Sports Medicine (AAPSM) or at least highly familiar with the needs and problems of distance runners. See **D.C.M.** and **M.D.**

Endurance Training Long distance jogging and running at an aerobic pace over a period of months and years, designed to improve the efficiency of the cardiovascular, pulmonary and metabolic systems. Also strengthens connective tissue and conditions the lower body muscles to long term, low intensity stress. See **Speed Training**.

Excuses Something everyone has lots of just before a race and the weekend twenty miler.

Even Pace See **Pace** and **Splits**.

Fun Run A community run usually held in a park. There are no qualifying times and people of all ages and abilities participate. They are usually from 2 miles to 6.2 miles (10 KM) in length.

Glue-Gun A simple electric device that melts plugs of resilient plastic. See **Hot-Melt-Glue**.

Glycogen A starch stored in muscle tissue that is the principal fuel for the muscle. It will not be shuted from muscle to muscle. See **Carbohydrate Loading**.

Heel Counter The part of your training flat or jogging shoe that cups the heel. It should be firm. See **Training Flat**.

Hot-Melt-Glue A resilient plastic used to keep the heels of training flats from running over and gradually throwing the foot-leg-hip system out of alignment. Thin applications of hot-melt-glue also retard wear in the ball area of the shoe. See **Glue-Gun**.

Intervals Relatively short, fast, consecutive runs alternated with periods or rest, walking or slow jogging to partial or complete recovery. See **Speed Training** and **Anaerobic Exercise**.

Jog A pace that's more than a walk but slower than you're really capable of. A comfortable running pace where you're unaware or not interested in time. Jogger: Not concerned with competition. See **Run**.

Jogging Shoe See **Training Flat**.

Junk Shoe It looks great (racing stripes, etc.) but has a mushy heel, hard sole and little padding, not much heel lift and is stiff. Stay away from it regardless of price. They are usually found in discount and department stores that do not necessarily cater to runners and joggers. See **Training Flat**.

The Perfect Marathon

King Kong A member of the West University Placers running team. They're not too fast, but they're big!

Leg-Ups An exercise that works directly on the lower part of the stomach. They should always be performed with the head and upper back flush with the ground or sit-up board. See **Sit-Ups**.

Limbering In particular the stretching and loosening of the front of the legs (quadriceps), the back of the legs (hamstrings and calves) and the lower back, but can also involve other parts of the body.

LSD Long Slow Distance training. Under the right circumstances can cause visions, strange sensations and mystical insights.

Marathon 1) An impossible event—no one can do it! 2) 26.2 miles of hell—it's even too far to drive! 3) Something to be experienced but never conquered. 4) Something you will attempt, experience, finish and remember for the rest of your life.

Marathon Predictor Chart There is a direct relationship between your best time at five miles and your potential in the marathon. Whether you are a highly trained fun runner or a world class competitor, the relationship between five mile times and marathon times is the same. The Predictor Chart turns this observable fact into a practical tool for closely estimating marathon potential.

M.D. Doctor. When in doubt, check with her or him. See **D.C.M.** and **D.P.M.**

Mileage Log Something you should fill in daily, whether you jog that day or not.

Moleskin A Dr. Scholl's product used to cover sore spots on the foot and line the heel counter of a running shoe for firmer fit.

Off Day A day in which you do some form of non-limb pounding exercise instead of running.

Pace The average per mile speed of a run over a given distance. Two minutes for the quarter mile would be an 8 minute mile pace. For the marathon distance, an even pace overall is technically the most efficient.

Pain Something to be avoided if at all possible. If encountered it should be dealt with right away—*do not run through pain*.

Peaking The point where you are in top physical, mental and emotional condition. This should occur as near as possible to race day. It is important not to peak too soon. See **Burn Out**.

Progressive Resistance Training A form of training using geared machines, weights or elastic cables, where the amount of resistance can be increased at a specific rate either during the exercise or over time. See **Weight Training**.

Racing Flat A running shoe designed primarily for light weight rather than support or shock absorption— there may be exceptions.

Replacement Drink A cool liquid taken during long training runs, marathons and just after finishing. They are designed to replace certain minerals/salts/electrolytes and sometimes sugars. I advise that highly sugared drinks not be taken until after the race. However plain water or highly diluted replacement drinks should be taken at every possible opportunity up 'til the 20 mile mark.

Road Runners of America The largest group of running clubs in the U.S.

Run More than a jog but less than racing. A pace in which you are concerned with time or exerting a little pressure on yourself. Runner: Someone who has a concern, no matter how slight, with times or racing.

Rubber Clothing Do not train while wearing rubber or plastic clothing. They will not help burn up fat but may cause a serious depletion of body fluids and salts and can bring on heat stroke. See **Weight Loss**.

Sit-Ups An exercise that helps strengthen the upper part of the stomach and aids in taking undue strain off the back. Sit-ups should always be performed with the legs bent.

Sleep 1. Something you'll probably need more of as training distances increase and intensity becomes greater—as much as 10 to 12 hours a night just prior to marathon. 2. Something you will probably be short of the night before your big race.

Speed Training A relatively short period (about six weeks or so) devoted to sharpening the body system for racing. See **Endurance Training.**

Splits Accumulated times given at set distances during a training session or race. In a marathon official splits are often given at 1 mile, 5 miles, 10, 15, 20 and 25 miles. Unofficially, splits are sometimes given at mile intervals. Split times are what makes even pacing practical and possible. See **Pace** and **Even Pace.**

Split Workout More than one running session in a day, usually morning and evening, but sometimes also including a noon session.

Stich A sharp stabbing pain or cramp under the ribs in the area of the diaphragm. Cause unknown. May be due to trapped gas or the result of forced breathing initiated by too fast a pace. Often can be helped by direct massage combined with a slower pace or walking and pinching the upper lip until it goes numb. See **Cramps.**

Stopwatch A device to measure time in hours, minutes, seconds and either 10ths or 100ths of a second. See **Chronometer.**

Training Flat A highly engineered, stable and shock absorbing shoe designed for distance training and jogging, and highly recommend by me for distance racing. See **Jogging Shoes, Junk Shoes** and **Racing Flats.**

Understanding What you'll need from loved ones once you begin training for hours at a time. See **Company.**

Vaseline A magic balm for runners that should be applied liberally to all areas that rub; especially the inner thighs, the nipples and under the arms. Some runners even grease their feet. Heavier runners will find that as they lose weight their thighs will chafe less, however chest chafing will always remain a problem for some men and women. If vaseline doesn't protect enough, Band-Aids may be applied directly over the nipples.

Walking 1. What you do before you learn to run. 2. What you use to get your breathing back to normal early in training. 3. What you use to cool-off after a jogging session.

Wall 1. An imaginary point in the marathon where someone drops a cow on your shoulders. 2. A deep muddy bog that begins around 18 to 20 miles into the marathon. 3. An absolutely vertical sand hill six miles from the finish. 4. A point where all around you people's legs turn to Jello, but where you (who have read *The Perfect Marathon*) feel a new burst of confidence and an overpowering will to finish in style.

Warm-down A low intensity exercise following a hard workout. See **Warm-up.**

Warm-up Any low intensity exercise or movements used to prepare the muscles for a similar exercise of greater intensity. See **Warm-down** and **Cool-off.**

Weight Gain During early stages of walking and jogging one sometimes gains weight because the activity is enough to enhance the appetite but not enough to burn a lot of calories. Later, it is possible for size to decrease while weight remains stable or even goes up a bit, because puffy fat is being replaced by firm, compact healthy tissue.

Weight Loss The results of long distance training (at least 3 miles three times a week) plus sensible eating habits are a firm, healthy, attractive body that will serve you well. Actual loss of weight will be slow, but changes in body makeup and appearance will be dramatic and rather swift. Do not be fooled by rapid weight loss as recorded directly after a run—this is usually the result of moderate dehydration. If dehydration is severe, urine will become dark . . . this can be a serious situation. See **Rubber Clothing.**

Weight Training A system of exercises that can apply a measured amount of resistence to a specific muscle or group of muscles without pounding the joints. This is usually a high intensity, relatively short duration form of exercise ideal as an adjunct to running. See **Progressive Resistance Training.**

Winner What you are as you run across the finish line of your first marathon. See **Marathon.**

The Marathon Predictor

Most marathon hopefuls go into their first race without the slightest clue as to their time capabilities in the event. Usually they have a plan like: ''I just want to finish—on my feet,'' or ''I want to go the distance without ever walking,'' or ''I'd like to at least break four hours,'' or ''Fred broke 3:30 the first time out, I guess I can do at least that well,'' and so on.

That's the way I went into my first marathon and that's the way my friends went into theirs. It's a wasteful, unproductive, unpleasant and often destructive method.

After examining the running records of thousands of marathon-trained athletes, from four hour plus novices to sub-2:30 national and world-class performers, it was discovered they all had some things in common—some obvious, some not obvious at all.

First, all runners can run one, three or five miles at a faster *pace* than they can for 26.2 miles. Distance affects everyone!

Secondly, there is a relationship between your best pace (under ideal conditions) for five or six miles and your best pace (again, ideal conditions) for the marathon.

Although we all have different five-mile times and different marathon times, the relationship between the two is pretty much the same for everyone, regardless of talent. Over distance we all slow down at about the same rate. What does this mean?

It means that given a formula expressing the rate of loss, a computer program can be written (if you're Jim Lindsey) converting five-mile time to marathon time. Thanks Jim.

The predictions on the chart are indications of fastest possible times under near-perfect conditions of environment and training. For example, if the course is hilly or if the weather is hot and humid, times will be slower. If you are running your first marathon, lack of experience is likely to cut into your pace. If you have run very few twenty-mile runs or if your weekly totals are low, again you will have to make adjustments. Weight is also an important factor and a roll of fat is bound to add seconds if not minutes to the finish.

At the beginning of *RUNNING THE RACE: Tactics* there's a questionnaire designed to allow you to customize the Marathon Predictor to your own state of training and to a particular race.

It's near impossible to overstate the value of the knowledge to be gained from the Predictor. To someone fresh, well-trained and excited at the start of a race, a few seconds—20 or 30—seem unimportant. Over 26.2 miles they add up to a lot. Knowing, for example, that you should average an 8:00 pace instead of forcing a 7:30 pace might very well make the difference between running a Perfect Marathon and not finishing at all. Of the men and women who enter marathons approximately 30% drop out before the end of the race. You don't have to be one of them.

The Marathon Predictor Chart

Actual 5 Mile Time (Pace)	Predicted Marathon Time (Pace)	5 Mile Time	10 Mile Time	15 Mile Time	20 Mile Time	25 Mile Time
25:00 (5:00)	2:24 (5:29)	0:27	0:54	1:22	1:49	2:17
25:15 (5:03)	2:25 (5:33)	0:27	0:55	1:23	1:51	2:18
25:30 (5:06)	2:27 (5:36)	0:28	0:56	1:24	1:52	2:20

(continued on following page)

The Marathon Predictor Chart (cont'd)

Actual 5 Mile Time (Pace)	Predicted Marathon Time (Pace)	5 Mile Time	10 Mile Time	15 Mile Time	20 Mile Time	25 Mile Time
25:45 (5:09)	2:28 (5:39)	0:28	0:56	1:24	1:53	2:21
26:00 (5:12)	2:29 (5:43)	0:28	0:57	1:25	1:54	2:22
26:15 (5:15)	2:31 (5:46)	0:28	0:57	1:26	1:55	2:24
26:30 (5:18)	2:32 (5:49)	0:29	0:58	1:27	1:56	2:25
26:45 (5:21)	2:34 (5:53)	0:29	0:58	1:28	1:57	2:27
27:00 (5:24)	2:35 (5:56)	0:29	0:59	1:29	1:58	2:28
27:15 (5:27)	2:37 (5:59)	0:29	0:59	1:29	1:59	2:29
27:30 (5:30)	2:38 (6:02)	0:30	1:00	1:30	2:00	2:31
27:45 (5:33)	2:40 (6:06)	0:30	1:01	1:31	2:02	2:32
28:00 (5:36)	2:41 (6:09)	0:30	1:01	1:32	2:03	2:33
28:15 (5:39)	2:42 (6:12)	0:31	1:02	1:33	2:04	2:35
28:30 (5:42)	2:44 (6:16)	0:31	1:02	1:34	2:05	2:36
28:45 (5:45)	2:45 (6:19)	0:31	1:03	1:34	2:06	2:38
29:00 (5:48)	2:47 (6:22)	0:31	1:03	1:35	2:07	2:39
29:15 (5:51)	2:48 (6:26)	0:32	1:04	1:36	2:08	2:40
29:30 (5:54)	2:50 (6:29)	0:32	1:04	1:37	2:09	2:42
29:45 (5:57)	2:51 (6:32)	0:32	1:05	1:38	2:10	2:43
30:00 (6:00)	2:53 (6:35)	0:32	1:05	1:38	2:11	2:44
30:15 (6:03)	2:54 (6:39)	0:33	1:06	1:39	2:13	2:46
30:30 (6:06)	2:55 (6:42)	0:33	1:07	1:40	2:14	2:47
30:45 (6:09)	2:57 (6:45)	0:33	1:07	1:41	2:15	2:49
31:00 (6:12)	2:58 (6:49)	0:34	1:08	1:42	2:16	2:50
31:15 (6:15)	3:00 (6:52)	0:34	1:08	1:43	2:17	2:51
31:30 (6:18)	3:01 (6:55)	0:34	1:09	1:43	2:18	2:53
31:45 (6:21)	3:03 (6:59)	0:34	1:09	1:44	2:19	2:54
32:00 (6:24)	3:04 (7:02)	0:35	1:10	1:45	2:20	2:55
32:15 (6:27)	3:06 (7:05)	0:35	1:10	1:46	2:21	2:57
32:30 (6:30)	3:07 (7:08)	0:35	1:11	1:47	2:22	2:58
32:45 (6:33)	3:08 (7:12)	0:36	1:12	1:48	2:24	3:00
33:00 (6:36)	3:10 (7:15)	0:36	1:12	1:48	2:25	3:01
33:15 (6:39)	3:11 (7:18)	0:36	1:13	1:49	2:26	3:02
33:30 (6:42)	3:13 (7:22)	0:36	1:13	1:50	2:27	3:04
33:45 (6:45)	3:14 (7:25)	0:37	1:14	1:51	2:28	3:05
34:00 (6:48)	3:16 (7:28)	0:37	1:14	1:52	2:29	3:06
34:15 (6:51)	3:17 (7:32)	0:37	1:15	1:53	2:30	3:08
34:30 (6:54)	3:18 (7:35)	0:37	1:15	1:53	2:31	3:09
34:45 (6:57)	3:20 (7:38)	0:38	1:16	1:54	2:32	3:11
35:00 (7:00)	3:21 (7:41)	0:38	1:16	1:55	2:33	3:12
35:15 (7:03)	3:23 (7:45)	0:38	1:17	1:56	2:35	3:13
35:30 (7:06)	3:24 (7:48)	0:39	1:18	1:57	2:36	3:15
35:45 (7:09)	3:26 (7:51)	0:39	1:18	1:57	2:37	3:16
36:00 (7:12)	3:27 (7:55)	0:39	1:19	1:58	2:38	3:17
36:15 (7:15)	3:29 (7:58)	0:39	1:19	1:59	2:39	3:19
36:30 (7:18)	3:30 (8:01)	0:40	1:20	2:00	2:40	3:20
36:45 (7:21)	3:31 (8:05)	0:40	1:20	2:01	2:41	3:22
37:00 (7:24)	3:33 (8:08)	0:40	1:21	2:02	2:42	3:23
37:15 (7:27)	3:34 (8:11)	0:40	1:21	2:02	2:43	3:24
37:30 (7:30)	3:36 (8:14)	0:41	1:22	2:03	2:44	3:26

(continued on following page)

179

The Marathon Predictor Chart (cont'd)

Actual 5 Mile Time (Pace)	Predicted Marathon Time (Pace)	5 Mile Time	10 Mile Time	15 Mile Time	20 Mile Time	25 Mile Time
37:45 (7:33)	3:37 (8:18)	0:41	1:23	2:04	2:46	3:27
38:00 (7:36)	3:39 (8:21)	0:41	1:23	2:05	2:47	3:28
38:15 (7:39)	3:40 (8:24)	0:42	1:24	2:06	2:48	3:30
38:30 (7:42)	3:42 (8:28)	0:42	1:24	2:07	2:49	3:31
38:45 (7:45)	3:43 (8:31)	0:42	1:25	2:07	2:50	3:33
39:00 (7:48)	3:44 (8:34)	0:42	1:25	2:08	2:51	3:34
39:15 (7:51)	3:46 (8:38)	0:43	1:26	2:09	2:52	3:35
39:30 (7:54)	3:47 (8:41)	0:43	1:26	2:10	2:53	3:37
39:45 (7:57)	3:49 (8:44)	0:43	1:27	2:11	2:54	3:38
40:00 (8:00)	3:50 (8:47)	0:43	1:27	2:11	2:55	3:39
40:15 (8:03)	3:52 (8:51)	0:44	1:28	2:12	2:57	3:41
40:30 (8:06)	3:53 (8:54)	0:44	1:29	2:13	2:58	3:42
40:45 (8:09)	3:55 (8:57)	0:44	1:29	2:14	2:59	3:44
41:00 (8:12)	3:56 (9:01)	0:45	1:30	2:15	3:00	3:45
41:15 (8:15)	3:57 (9:04)	0:45	1:30	2:16	3:01	3:46
41:30 (8:18)	3:59 (9:07)	0:45	1:31	2:16	3:02	3:48
41:45 (8:21)	4:00 (9:11)	0:45	1:31	2:17	3:03	3:49
42:00 (8:24)	4:02 (9:14)	0:46	1:32	2:18	3:04	3:50
42:15 (8:27)	4:03 (9:17)	0:46	1:32	2:19	3:05	3:52
42:30 (8:30)	4:05 (9:20)	0:46	1:33	2:20	3:06	3:53
42:45 (8:33)	4:06 (9:24)	0:47	1:34	2:21	3:08	3:55
43:00 (8:36)	4:08 (9:27)	0:47	1:34	2:21	3:09	3:56
43:15 (8:39)	4:09 (9:30)	0:47	1:35	2:22	3:10	3:57
43:30 (8:42)	4:10 (9:34)	0:47	1:35	2:23	3:11	3:59
43:45 (8:45)	4:12 (9:37)	0:48	1:36	2:24	3:12	4:00
44:00 (8:48)	4:13 (9:40)	0:48	1:36	2:25	3:13	4:01
44:15 (8:51)	4:15 (9:44)	0:48	1:37	2:26	3:14	4:03
44:30 (8:54)	4:16 (9:47)	0:48	1:37	2:26	3:15	4:04
44:45 (8:57)	4:18 (9:50)	0:49	1:38	2:27	3:16	4:06
45:00 (9:00)	4:19 (9:53)	0:49	1:38	2:28	3:17	4:07
45:15 (9:03)	4:21 (9:57)	0:49	1:39	2:29	3:19	4:08
45:30 (9:06)	4:22 (10:00)	0:50	1:40	2:30	3:20	4:10
45:45 (9:09)	4:23 (10:03)	0:50	1:40	2:30	3:21	4:11
46:00 (9:12)	4:25 (10:07)	0:50	1:41	2:31	3:22	4:12
46:15 (9:15)	4:26 (10:10)	0:50	1:41	2:32	3:23	4:14
46:30 (9:18)	4:28 (10:13)	0:51	1:42	2:33	3:24	4:15
46:45 (9:21)	4:29 (10:17)	0:51	1:42	2:34	3:25	4:17
47:00 (9:24)	4:31 (10:20)	0:51	1:43	2:35	3:26	4:18
47:15 (9:27)	4:32 (10:23)	0:51	1:43	2:35	3:27	4:19
47:30 (9:30)	4:33 (10:26)	0:52	1:44	2:36	3:28	4:21
47:45 (9:33)	4:35 (10:30)	0:52	1:45	2:37	3:30	4:22
48:00 (9:36)	4:36 (10:33)	0:52	1:45	2:38	3:31	4:23
48:15 (9:39)	4:38 (10:36)	0:53	1:46	2:39	3:32	4:25
48:30 (9:42)	4:39 (10:40)	0:53	1:46	2:40	3:33	4:26
48:45 (9:45)	4:41 (10:43)	0:53	1:47	2:40	3:34	4:28
49:00 (9:48)	4:42 (10:46)	0:53	1:47	2:41	3:35	4:29
49:15 (9:51)	4:44 (10:50)	0:54	1:48	2:42	3:36	4:30
49:30 (9:54)	4:45 (10:53)	0:54	1:48	2:43	3:37	4:32
49:45 (9:57)	4:46 (10:56)	0:54	1:49	2:44	3:38	4:33
50:00 (10:00)	4:48 (10:59)	0:54	1:49	2:44	3:39	4:34

Pace Chart

   If you wish to run at a specific pace per mile, this chart will enable you to check the accuracy of your pace at quarter mile intervals. In addition I have included the approximate marathon that would be achieved if that pace were continued for 26.2 miles.

Quarter Mile Pace	Per Mile x (4) =	Approximate Marathon Pace x (26.2) = Time	Quarter Mile Pace	Per Mile x (4) =	Approximate Marathon Pace x (26.2) = Time
1:15	5:00	2:11:06	1:55	7:40	3:21:01
1:16	5:04	2:12:51	1:56	7:44	3:22:46
1:17	5:08	2:14:36	1:57	7:48	3:24:32
1:18	5:12	2:16:21	1:58	7:52	3:26:17
1:19	5:16	2:18:06	1:59	7:56	3:28:00
1:20	5:20	2:19:50	2:00	8:00	3:29:45
1:21	5:24	2:21:35	2:01	8:04	3:31:31
1:22	5:28	2:23:20	2:02	8:08	3:33:16
1:23	5:32	2:25:05	2:03	8:12	3:35:01
1:24	5:36	2:26:50	2:04	8:16	3:36:46
1:25	5:40	2:28:34	2:05	8:20	3:38:30
1:26	5:44	2:30:19	2:06	8:24	3:40:14
1:27	5:48	2:32:04	2:07	8:28	3:41:59
1:28	5:52	2:33:49	2:08	8:32	3:43:46
1:29	5:56	2:35:34	2:09	8:36	3:45:32
1:30	6:00	2:37:19	2:10	8:40	3:47:13
1:31	6:04	2:39:04	2:11	8:44	3:48:58
1:32	6:08	2:40:49	2:12	8:48	3:50:43
1:33	6:12	2:42:34	2:13	8:52	3:52:28
1:34	6:16	2:44:19	2:14	8:56	3:54:13
1:35	6:20	2:46:03	2:15	9:00	3:55:58
1:36	6:24	2:47:48	2:16	9:04	3:57:43
1:37	6:28	2:49:33	2:17	9:08	3:59:28
1:38	6:32	2:51:18	2:18	9:12	4:01:13
1:39	6:36	2:53:03	2:19	9:16	4:02:59
1:40	6:40	2:54:47	2:20	9:20	4:04:44
1:41	6:44	2:56:32	2:21	9:24	4:06:29
1:42	6:48	2:58:17	2:22	9:28	4:06:14
1:43	6:52	3:00:02	2:23	9:32	4:07:59
1:44	6:56	3:01:47	2:24	9:36	4:09:44
1:45	7:00	3:03:33	2:25	9:40	4:13:27
1:46	7:04	3:05:18	2:26	9:44	4:15:12
1:47	7:08	3:07:03	2:27	9:48	4:16:57
1:48	7:12	3:08:47	2:28	9:52	4:18:42
1:49	7:16	3:10:32	2:29	9:56	4:21:27
1:50	7:20	3:12:17	2:30	10:00	4:22:11
1:51	7:24	3:14:02	2:31	10:04	4:23:56
1:52	7:28	3:15:47	2:32	10:08	4:25:41
1:53	7:32	3:17:33	2:33	10:12	4:27:26
1:54	7:36	3:19:18	2:34	10:16	4:29:11

Training Log: 7-Day/4-Week Schedule

WEEK 1

	DAY 1		DAY 2		DAY 3		DAY 4		DAY 5		DAY 6		DAY 7		7 DAY TOTAL
Daily Mileage															
Comments															
	AM	PM	AM	PM	AM	PM	AM	PM	AM	PM	AM	PM	AM	PM	WEIGHT
Pulse															

WEEK 2

	DAY 1		DAY 2		DAY 3		DAY 4		DAY 5		DAY 6		DAY 7		7 DAY TOTAL
Daily Mileage															
Comments															
	AM	PM	AM	PM	AM	PM	AM	PM	AM	PM	AM	PM	AM	PM	WEIGHT
Pulse															

Training Log: 7-Day/4-Week Schedule

WEEK 3

	DAY 1		DAY 2		DAY 3		DAY 4		DAY 5		DAY 6		DAY 7		7 DAY TOTAL
	AM	PM	AM	PM	AM	PM	AM	PM	AM	PM	AM	PM	AM	PM	
Daily Mileage															
Comments															WEIGHT
Pulse															

WEEK 4

	DAY 1		DAY 2		DAY 3		DAY 4		DAY 5		DAY 6		DAY 7		7 DAY TOTAL
	AM	PM	AM	PM	AM	PM	AM	PM	AM	PM	AM	PM	AM	PM	
Daily Mileage															
Comments															WEIGHT
Pulse															

Training Log: 7-Day/4-Week Schedule

WEEK 1

	DAY 1	DAY 2	DAY 3	DAY 4	DAY 5	DAY 6	DAY 7	7 DAY TOTAL
Daily Mileage								
Comments								WEIGHT
Pulse	AM | PM	AM | PM	AM | PM	AM | PM	AM | PM	AM | PM	AM | PM	

WEEK 2

	DAY 1	DAY 2	DAY 3	DAY 4	DAY 5	DAY 6	DAY 7	7 DAY TOTAL
Daily Mileage								
Comments								WEIGHT
Pulse	AM | PM	AM | PM	AM | PM	AM | PM	AM | PM	AM | PM	AM | PM	

Training Log: 7-Day/4-Week Schedule

WEEK 3

	DAY 1	DAY 2	DAY 3	DAY 4	DAY 5	DAY 6	DAY 7	7 DAY TOTAL
Daily Mileage								
Comments								
Pulse	AM / PM	AM / PM	AM / PM	AM / PM	AM / PM	AM / PM	AM / PM	WEIGHT

WEEK 4

	DAY 1	DAY 2	DAY 3	DAY 4	DAY 5	DAY 6	DAY 7	7 DAY TOTAL
Daily Mileage								
Comments								
Pulse	AM / PM	AM / PM	AM / PM	AM / PM	AM / PM	AM / PM	AM / PM	WEIGHT

You can have your very own copy of *The Perfect Marathon* by Michael Schreiber to keep or give to a fellow runner by filling out the form below and sending it along with your check to:

John Muir Publications
P.O. Box 613
Santa Fe, NM 87501

Name _____

Address _____

City _____ State _____ Zip _____

Please send me____copies of *The Perfect Marathon* @ $7.50 each _____

Postage ($1.00 for the first copy, 25¢ for each additional copy)......_____

Tax, if you live in sunny New Mexico, @ 32¢ per copy..................._____

Total enclosed ...._____

Michael Schreiber is available for speaking engagements and lecture tours.
Contact John Muir Publications for further information.